Eval p 142

INTERNATIONAL TEXTBOOKS IN ART EDUCATION

Italo L. de Francesco

Consulting Editor

TEACHING
SECONDARY
ART

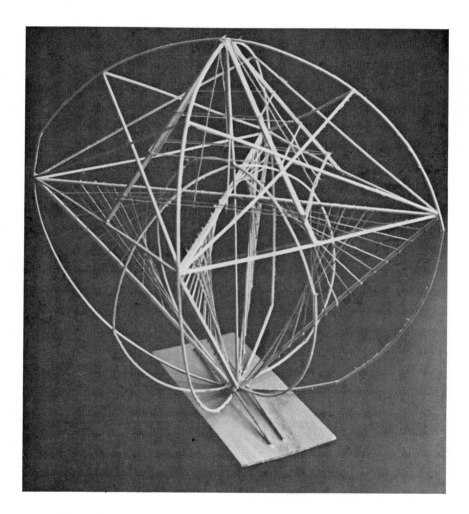

Balsa, reed, and yarn three-dimensional construction by a senior high school student. (Courtesy of Kansas City, Missouri, Public Schools.)

TEACHING
SECONDARY
ART

VINCENT LANIER

INTERNATIONAL TEXTBOOK COMPANY

Scranton, Pennsylvania

126940

For the ultimate aim of education is nothing other than the creation of human beings in the fullness of their capacities. Through the making of human beings, of men and women generous in aspiration, liberal in thought, cultivated in taste, and equipped with knowledge and competent method, society itself is constantly remade, and with this remaking the world itself is recreated.

—JOHN DEWEY

Preface

The material in this volume was developed to serve as a textbook in secondary art education courses in teacher training institutions and as a reference source for teachers and administrative and supervisory personnel in local school districts and larger units of our educational system. The text and illustrative materials attempt to analyze the various components of the secondary art program in sufficient depth to act as a guide to the selection of aims, curriculum, and methodology.

To the extent that this is desirable, a range of points of view are often presented. This is not to suggest either that all approaches to art education are equally viable or that the author wishes to remain uncommitted. It is assumed, simply, that the art of teaching art, or any other subject area, is presently a largely subjective enterprise about which there is far too little relevant reliable information. It is assumed, therefore, that the reader will select his particular preference among the viewpoints presented within the limits imposed by the democratic context in which all our schools operate.

In this sense, this volume does not assert any "ideal" curriculum or methodology to be copied or used by the reader. The examples selected are tested and effective and should be of help in stimulating ideas about the art program in the secondary schools.

Also, the proper distinction between junior and senior high school will be largely eliminated for the purposes of this volume. While art curricula and methods on each level have legitimate and characteristic differences, the purpose here is not to describe what art programs are or should be, but rather, how they are and should be conceived and designed. In this sense, there is no substantial distinction between junior and senior high school.

Portions of this book have been carefully documented in an effort to bring to the reader the widest possible range of names and sources in the literature of art education and other literature relevant to art education. It it hoped, of course, that reading these pages will stimulate the art education student or teacher or lay reader to further investigation into the ideas of the field.

Most good things made by man are the result of thought, either shared group thought or, more commonly, individual thought. This volume cannot replace the imaginative, thoughtful student, teacher, or supervisor. However, it might prove of some value in helping to structure the thinking and stimulate the imagination of those concerned with secondary art.

VINCENT LANIER

Los Angeles, California
March, 1964

Contents

List of Illustrations

List of Tables and Forms

I

The Secondary Art Program

The study of a specific subject area in education poses several problems, related but sufficiently discrete to be studied individually. Traditionally, these problems have been the questions of aims, curriculum, and methodology. However, from the point of view of a beginning teacher or an experienced teacher in a new situation, certain other factors of major significance must be recognized.

Therefore, the choice and sequence of the materials in this volume reflect desirable procedures to be used by the teacher in organizing a program of art in the secondary school. From the first chapter analysis of the present status of secondary art education to the last chapter examination of secondary art methodology, each step and its position is presented as closely as possible in the chronological order in which one might actually plan an educational program in this field.

Inevitably, this process leads to some fragmentation and repetition. For example, somewhat arbitrary distinctions are made between curriculum and methodology or between motivation and presentation, which are in truth much more closely related. These ruptures, while essential for analysis, present a less coherent picture of secondary art education than one might wish.

PRESENT ROLE OF SECONDARY ART

A reasonable starting point for the purposes of this volume is an examination of the present status of art in the secondary schools.

The next steps in this chapter involve an analysis of the difficulties which may be encountered in organizing an art program and a brief overview of the principles of curriculum construction. Methodology, which is most commonly concerned with actual classroom procedure, is left to a later chapter.

A 1951 bulletin of the U.S. Office of Education informs us that, "Art subjects are pursued much less frequently by pupils in the upper years of the secondary school."[1] The bulletin reports that while 48 per cent of all junior high school pupils enroll in art classes, only 10 per cent of senior high school and 13 per cent of combined secondary school pupils take art courses.

Twelve years later, Hastie and Templeton in the report of a study carried on at the University of Minnesota indicate that, during the period 1957-1963, while art programs flourished on the elementary and junior high school levels, senior high school art seemed to be losing ground. In comparing enrollments, for example, the authors state that, ". . . we find over three times as many of the high schools showing a decrease in enrollments as that of the junior highs."[2]

The pattern for art enrollment described in these surveys indicates the tendency in our educational systems to require art or a choice between art and another subject (most often music, industrial arts, or home economics) or a split term of ten weeks of art and ten weeks of music on the junior high school level, while maintaining no requirement of art in the senior high school.

In contrast to these findings, an NEA Research Monograph (M3 1963) on *Music and Art in the Public Schools* reflecting a sampling of almost 700 secondary schools, shows a slight increase in art enrollments. The NEA data, compiled over approximately the same time span as the

[1] "Offerings and Enrollments in High School Subjects," *Biennial Survey of Education in the United States, 1948-1950* (Washington, D.C.: Federal Security Agency, Office of Education, 1951), p. 25.

[2] Reid Hastie and David Templeton, "Art Education in the Secondary Schools," *Research Report 1-63* (Minneapolis, Minn.: University of Minnesota, 1963), p. 4.

Hastie and Templeton study, reveals a greater increase in senior high school art enrollments than in junior high school art enrollments, thus to some extent reversing the University of Minnesota findings. However, the totals involved in the NEA report suggest ample cause for concern about the scope of art in American secondary schools. Only 53.6 per cent of the secondary schools responding to the survey offered any art at all, and though 96.5 per cent of the large secondary schools offered art at the senior high level, only 14.9 per cent of their students enrolled in art classes during the 1961-62 school year.

Many small high schools have no art electives at all, and the larger schools vary in their offerings from a limited few classes to "major" curricula, occasionally on a pre-professional level. Generally, however, it appears that most of our young people have no substantial classroom experience in the visual arts beyond the junior high school years. Furthermore, it must be admitted that despite some excellent experimental secondary programs and some symptoms of an increase in interest in the arts over the nation, there would seem to be no discernable force influencing public education towards an increase in secondary art offerings. It can only be hoped that world and national events and the dedicated activities of art educators will eventually have the desired impact on the schools.

Even without a growth in scope, however, the selection of courses and course content, and the determination of methodology present substantial difficulties for the administrator, supervisor, or teacher of art in the secondary schools. This problem is most clearly observable when one examines the literature of art education, in which the wealth of existing material offers little if any direction in precisely what factors do or should influence decision making in the curriculum. The more popular periodicals in the field present an incessant barrage of new materials and processes. General textbooks in art education make rather vague and inconclusive remarks about creativity and aesthetic growth. Researchers in the universities glean fragments of uncoordinated knowledge. No one seems willing to offer a comprehensive, positive approach to the secondary art curriculum.

The picture in elementary art, on the other hand, is in sharp, almost startling, contrast. A number of volumes—rightly or wrongly—suggest specific organizations of particular activities. In fact, there is so much material that one might almost say that elementary art literature is overcrowded.

Figure 1   *Head,* plaster and vermiculite sculpture by a tenth grade pupil. (Courtesy of University School, Florida State University.)

DIFFICULTIES IN DEVELOPING THE ART CURRICULUM

Reasons for the dearth of secondary art curriculum materials are not difficult to name. First of all, the critical awareness of the adolescent's approach to art—particularly on a productive level—raises significant difficulties in the study and analysis of his art behavior. A developmental pattern by which curriculum can be structured is far more difficult to isolate on this level than in the case of the elementary child. Secondly, there is a lack of interest at the secondary level because of its numerical limitation. After all, art of some sort is part of the school life of most children from kindergarten through sixth grade, and the majority of classroom teachers have some kind of pre-service training in art education. However, secondary art is a confined area and cannot support an extensive literature. Thirdly, while art can easily function as one aspect of a multi-faceted elementary curriculum, its position on the secondary level is isolated, as a separate subject, tending to focus the confusions in the field on that level.

In a recent analysis of art programs in the secondary schools, Barkan[3] sees the major stumbling blocks to an adequate development of art curricula on this level as the ignorance of school authorities with respect to the essential values of humanistic experiences, improper guidance practices leading to the enrollment of unmotivated or unprepared pupils, ineffectual scheduling patterns of inflexible period lengths, insufficient school time in which the art teacher can develop instructional materials, and inappropriate space, equipment, facilities, and resource materials.

The number and seriousness of these confusions are considerable, although they have impact only within the field. Krug comments interestingly on this situation, noting that while there is active controversial discussion of issues of importance to the field among art teachers, few school people outside the field are even aware of its problems. Teachers in other subject areas might welcome such acceptance since their own subjects are too much in the public eye. However, the lack of recognition of problems may well be due to indifference rather than acceptance.[4] There would seem to be little doubt in the minds of many

---

[3] Manuel Barkan, "The Visual Arts in Secondary School Education," *The School Review*, Vol. 70, No. 4 (1962), pp. 457-472.

[4] Edward A. Krug, *The Secondary School Curriculum* (New York: Harper & Brothers, 1960), p. 342.

art educators—and none in the mind of the author—that indifference is by far the more accurate of the two terms.

Chapter II of this volume will attempt to identify some of the issues presently being debated in the area of art education. For the moment, it is sufficient to assert that the lack of coherent analysis of the general functions of school art, both intrinsic and instrumental, is perhaps the prime reason for the uncertain condition of secondary curricula in art. Hampered in his thinking by confusion as to what art can do for pupils, and threatened to the point of increasing urgency by the call for a return to so-called intellectual disciplines, the secondary art teacher often finds it difficult to sustain his toehold in the door of the high school, much less to advance the importance of art in the curriculum.

Figure 2   Silver rings, senior high school. (Courtesy of Pasadena, California, City Schools.)

Munro[5] also testifies to this confusion, pointing to one contemporary aspect:

> Art teachers tend to divide into two main camps: first, the so-called "progressive" wing, favoring comparative freedom for the student, a psychological and sociological approach, and integration rather than the subject curriculum; secondly, the more conservative wing, sometimes called "academic," favoring more discipline, re-

[5] Thomas Munro, *Art Education: Its Philosophy and Psychology* (New York: The Liberal Arts Press, 1956), pp. 29-30.

quired knowledge and technique, and more intensive, directed, systematic study of a limited realm of art.

While most teachers, Munro feels, represent a fair middle point between the two extremes, "Nevertheless vigorous disputes still arise over details of method and content."

Krug[6] offers a sustained and definitive analysis of the problems of the high school art curriculum, bringing out several problems in addition to the basic one of confusion in theories. The change in the nature of student response to school activities is another factor. "The apparent decline of spontaneous creativity in the adolescent years is a point difficult to pin down. Perhaps it is only folklore, but teachers in all fields testify to its existence."[7]

The size of many of our high schools serves to limit the range of art programs, a point made by Conant[8] in his recent survey, though not specifically with reference to art. Many art activities require extensive and expensive equipment, necessitating a large expenditure for a small number of children, a burden our culture is unaccountably reluctant to assume.

While specialized art courses taken on an elective basis or for a major program are easy to defend, proposing the addition of a general art course in high school raises a further problem. If the purpose of such a course is to promote appreciation of and interest in art, why would not a seventh- or eighth-grade course following an effective elementary art program satisfy the need?

Again, instead of a general art course, advanced specialized courses could be made a requirement in order to promote the interest of capable pupils. An adequate elementary and junior high level program should have supplied this development.

However, other curriculum areas warrant required high school courses. Why should not the visual arts be accorded the same stress? The answer seems to lie in the insistence of art education people on the need for studio activities as the primary means of attaining their objectives. Only English and physical education presently insist on such a program of continued skill development, and this would be the only argument the visual arts might advance.

A further consideration of relevance to this matter is the somewhat parochial attitude among many in art education that the child will

[6] Krug, *op. cit.*, pp. 341-358.
[7] *Ibid.*, p. 346.
[8] James B. Conant, *The American High School Today* (New York: McGraw-Hill Book Company, Inc., 1959).

be cheated of opportunities to develop aesthetic insight if he has no specific required curricular experiences in the fine arts.

But responsibility for the aesthetic objectives need not be centered in the department of visual arts. Other fields of instruction, particularly music, industrial arts, physical education, English, and foreign languages deal with subject matter and activities directly related to aesthetics. Some subjects, such as mathematics, usually not thought of as among the arts, are in actuality far from irrelevant to the development of aesthetic insight and understanding.[9]

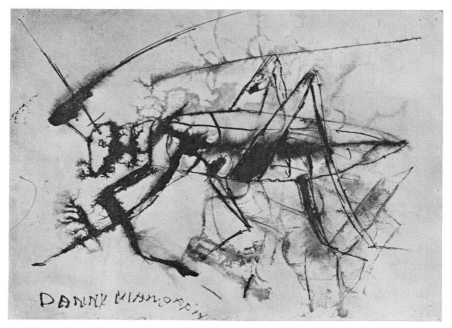

Figure 3   *The Grasshopper*, pen, brush, and ink drawing by a junior high school pupil. (Courtesy of Long Beach, California, City Schools.)

Krug concludes his analysis with several minimal suggestions including one year of required art on the junior high level, one year of required art in the senior high school for those who have not experienced a thorough program prior to ninth or tenth grade, the widest possible program of elective course offerings, and a change in the four-subjects-at-a-time tradition so that more subjects now only elective can be taken in the senior high school.

[9] Krug, *op. cit.*, p. 356.

Despite the number of complex problems, art courses and course content are being planned and taught each day in our schools. It is to be hoped that this planning is done according to some type of systematically organized criteria. While art education itself has no concise and detailed criteria, general curriculum materials offer suggestions as to how courses and content can be selected and organized.

Broadly conceived, there are two approaches to curriculum design, one being subject matter oriented, the other being pupil oriented.[10] In the first, the curriculum is organized according to *a priori* conceptions of significant subject disciplines, decisions made by teachers, administrators, supervisors, or even higher officials as to the "need" for specific content without reference to the context of the particular situation. To some extent, all educational institutions responsible to the several states must, at least initially, structure their curricula on the basis of requirements mandated by the state. The curriculum requirements of the New York State Board of Regents, and the requirements of English, American History, and so forth of state departments of education in other states, are examples of this aspect of subject matter orientation.

The second and contrasting approach, that of the pupil-oriented path, purports to construct curricula according to an assessment of the needs and interests of the particular group of pupils for whom the curriculum is being designed. In this approach, course content and courses, where possible, grow out of the particular educational context.

The secondary art program, rarely mandated by the states, has a far greater degree of flexibility than many sister subjects. Nevertheless, the two broad approaches are still possible in art curriculum design, the first conceiving of certain art experiences as essential to all pupils on a particular level, the second looking to the pupils and their learning environment to discover significant art experiences.

This volume has been written from a point of view somewhat

[10] F. B. Stratemeyer, H. L. Forkner, and M. G. McKim, *Developing a Curriculum for Modern Living* (New York: Teachers College, Columbia University, 1947), p. 6.

All educators recognize the need for school experiences which will develop individuals able to take a responsible place in our society. Yet some educators hold that these experiences should stem directly and wholly from the expressed needs and interests of the learners; others would start with these needs but would assume responsibility for pointing up new needs, developing new interests, and widening understandings; while a third group sees in the learner's immaturity little to give guidance in the selection of experiences and make this almost entirely the responsibility of the adults guiding his education. And there are points of view in between these three major positions.

closer to the second position than the first. It is granted, however, as
the chapter on values will indicate, that some degree of cultural generalization is valid and necessary. It seems entirely reasonable to assume
that inside the political boundaries of the United States certain objectives in art should be attempted for all children. It also seems defensible,
however, to select the one experience among alternative experiences
that will promote the attainment of each of these objectives on the
basis of the needs, interests, and particular environment of groups of
pupils. In other words, it might be said that within a culture all children of a particular age level share a broad common base of needs and
interests. While this may be difficult to visualize in art, it should be
quite apparent in English, for example. In one sense, in terms of this
argument, curriculum design from either of the two major orientations
would achieve similar broad fundamentals.

The issue in art is further complicated by the fact, observed by
some, that the visual arts do not presently possess any properly conceived subject matter as does science, mathematics, or social studies.

> The subject matter of the fine arts, drawn from many fields, is
> neither highly systematized nor standardized at any of the levels of
> education. In selecting and organizing the subject matters, interests
> and the maturity levels of the pupils serve as the main criteria.
> Thus, a ninth-grader with no background in art and a fourth-grader
> who studied art in second and third grades might be able to handle
> the same subject matter. The subject matter is determined largely by
> the needs of the individual pupil as they are revealed to the teacher,
> not, as in the case with mathematics, upon a progressively increased
> level of difficulty arbitrarily settled in terms of grade levels.[11]

Attempts to devise such basic subject materials have been numerous.[12]
However, it must be admitted that there is no substantial agreement
among art educators on any one format.

GENERAL PRINCIPLES OF CURRICULUM DESIGN

During this century, the general area of curriculum design has
developed into a major educational problem. In a less sophisticated
period, curriculum could be easily rationalized on the basis of 1) certain
fundamental disciplines that promoted the ability to think, such as
mathematics and language; 2) differences in social need, such as an

[11] James M. Hughes, *Education in America* (Evanston, Ill.: Row, Peterson & Company, 1960), p. 410.
[12] See Reed, Wickiser, and state and school district art guides listed in the appendices.

Figure 4   *Still Life*, charcoal drawing by an eleventh grade pupil. (Courtesy of Honolulu Academy of Arts, Honolulu, Hawaii.)

academic emphasis for middle-class pupils and vocational stress for children from lower income groups; or 3) the limited function of the school in that its role was confined to teaching particular skills and knowledges.

As our insights into the psychology of learning deepened and egalitarianism and social mobility advanced, the schools accepted a larger nominal share in the total training of the young, and the curriculum became an increasingly complex and sensitive concern. It appears as if only the constant of cultural lag and the accumulation of vested interests held the structure of curriculum in the American schools as firm as it has been. Today in the United States, the popular demand for a return to a more elemental curriculum may possibly retrace the direction of our recent growth. This is at least problematical. Suffice it to say that the present professional attitude toward curriculum design is by no means lucid or concise. One authoritative source states:

> Few problems in the field of education are more complex and controversial than those to which this chapter is addressed. What is the nature and what is the function of subject matter in the instructional program of the high school? What is the source of curriculum content? On what basis should it be selected? In what fashion should it be organized? There are no simple, direct answers to these difficult questions and none will be attempted here.[13]

In discussing a recent curriculum guide, the authors of a general education textbook describe the sections of the guide as a description of social and economic conditions in the particular community, a survey of purposes of public education in America, principles and practices in child growth and development, and chapters on specific curriculum areas.[14] The same textbook lists the determinants of the curriculum as: *a*) the influence of teacher and pupils, *b*) social influences, and *c*) the influence of the school's organization.[15]

Barkan sees the "working situation" as having five major components: *a*) the community, *b*) the general curriculum, *c*) the physical conditions, *d*) the children with their habits and attitudes, and *e*) the teacher.[16]

---

[13] Arno A. Bellack, "Selection and Organization of Curriculum Content: An Analysis," *What Shall the High Schools Teach,* 1956 Yearbook, Association for Supervision and Curriculum Development, p. 97.

[14] L. G. Thomas, L. B. Kinney, A. P. Coladarci, and H. E. Fielstra, *Perspective on Teaching* (Englewood Cliffs, N.J.: Prentice-Hall, Inc., 1961), p. 65.

[15] *Ibid.*, pp. 70-77.

[16] Manuel Barkan, *A Foundation for Art Education* (New York: The Ronald Press, 1955), p. 204.

A recent art education textbook contains the following generalized suggestions, listed in the chapter entitled, "Improving the School Art Program."

> Preliminary to any plan of improvement should be a carefully organized survey of existing conditions. For example,
> 1. During a period of two or three weeks, obtain an overview of the entire school-community situation. Look beyond everyday details to see major patterns in the curriculum, the underlying philosophy of the staff, and characteristics of the community.
> 2. Gather facts and organize them into appropriate categories. Study existing literature on the local situation as well as related professional writings. . . .[17]

It would be reasonable to assert that curricula in a particular subject area are usually designed on the basis of these or similar considerations. The factors deemed important may be stated in different ways or may include a greater number of varieties of specific influences. The most valuable statement would more than likely be the most general one.

In general terms, therefore, the design of a curriculum can be said to be dependent upon four major considerations:

1. The educational environment—the pupils, the school, and the community.
2. The educational aims—both the general goals of the particular culture and the specific objectives in a subject area.
3. The content which is available to implement the desired outcomes.
4. The methodology used to bring the content to the pupils in order to accomplish the aims.

Ideally, the teacher, supervisor, administrator, or other person responsible for curriculum structure should have access to the most recent information about the first three aspects of the specific situation. Without full knowledge of these elements, which might be said to be the WHO, WHY, and WHAT of the situation, a curriculum cannot reflect the kind of preparation most consonant with the tradition of education in the United States.

If we add to this list a fourth element, the consideration of method, or the HOW of the situation, a complete description of an art program can be developed.

[17] Howard Conant and Arne Randall, *Art in Education* (Peoria, Ill.: Charles A. Bennett, 1959), pp. 276-277.

Figure 5　*Western Scene*, mixed media drawing and painting done with tempera paints and inks by a high school senior. (Courtesy of Pasadena, California, City Schools.)

Although these elements are listed in a particular sequence, the order is not meant to suggest a necessary chronology of actions. It is reasonable to assume that the curriculum designer will bring to any school situation general concepts of desirable direction or, in educational language, general objectives already predetermined by the culture in which he has matured and by his teacher training experiences. Thus, the sequence of action will often be different from that listed here.

In some cases, particularly with those teachers most heavily preoccupied with the subject they are teaching, a curriculum design is formulated on top of concerns with particular materials. In the art program, for example, the teacher who is absorbed in his own painting or potting or printmaking may bring to the curriculum his primary concern with a specific art medium. In this instance, too, the order of action will be different, content considerations coming before the other elements.

In order to analyze the construction of a curriculum, however, it is not only useful but also necessary to delineate arbitrary distinctions and sequences of procedure. Another example is to be found in the common jurisdictional division between content and method, as is to be found in courses in teacher training institutions. It is extremely difficult, if not impossible, to draw a clearly defined line between content and method. The WHAT is theoretically and operationally intermingled with the HOW. In universities and in this volume also, the distinction will be maintained in order to present ideas with the maximum clarity and coherence.

Each of the four major elements mentioned warrants careful analysis. The intent of this volume, therefore, is to examine these areas with attention to historical background and appropriate illustrative detail. Sample curriculum and methodological materials and photographs have been chosen to exemplify what some teachers in the United States have done and are doing in representative educational situations. The reader is reminded again that all of these materials as well as the text are presented here as "A" method of procedure rather than "THE" method of procedure in curriculum design.

A further word might be said on the subject of cooperative pupil-teacher planning and the individualized curriculum. From the foregoing discussion it would appear that teachers, supervisors, or administrators undertake the total planning of course and course content without reference to the wishes or judgments of the pupils. Not only is this not always the case, but there is considerable developmental value in encouraging the participation of both junior and senior high school pupils in the planning of course content. Indeed, it is one other way in which the schools can inculcate democratic habits in social relationships, which constitute both our children's heritage and their hope for the future.

Reed offers one technique of cooperative planning for the junior high school level, which is traditionally sound in its format and can be generalized for the entire secondary level.

> Here is a proved method of developing an outline of a series of units with the pupils:
> (1) On the chalkboard, make a list of the art areas in which the students indicate interest. (2) Through discussion, point up the various information, skill, and design elements incorporated. Then (3) a comprehensive outline for a semester's or year's activities can be developed on the board. Students will appreciate this opportunity to organize their own course. They will know what areas they are to explore and will anticipate with pleasure projects which have personal appeal.
> Of course, the teacher has the responsibility of being sure that adequate emphasis is placed on units which will be of most benefit to the over-all plan and of suggesting units which might be overlooked by the students due to lack of background experiences.[18]

The benefits of such a scheme in terms of increased pupil interest are quite obvious. However, it should be equally obvious that there are serious limitations to this type of planning. First of all, the problem of supplies in secondary art is critical in nature. It is virtually impossible to conduct an effective art program without adequate art materials. The entire financial and distributive organization of the secondary schools makes it imperative that the art teacher order his supplies well in advance of a particular activity, usually once or twice a year. In order to do this, the art teacher must have some reasonably precise notion of the nature and quantity of those supplies, most commonly necessitating his own planning of the curriculum prior to his contact with the pupils who are to use the materials he is ordering.

Secondly, many worth-while art materials and techniques may be unknown to many pupils. It would be rather fruitless to ask youngsters to make judgments based upon less-than-adequate information. Also,

[18] Carl Reed, *Early Adolescent Art Education* (Peoria, Ill.: Charles A. Bennett Co., 1957), p. 82.

unless a poll is taken on each suggestion—which usually tends to destroy the spontaneity of the action—class planning often becomes a representation of the desires or opinions of the most articulate members of the group. The utmost skill and care are required of the teacher who attempts this type of planning.

A frequent compromise solution to these problems involves the use of a free-choice activity during one or several continuous or separate periods. Another typical compromise is the selection of individual subject matter by the pupils, to be done with required materials. While both of these approaches are by no means similar to cooperative planning, they do provide some of the desired benefits while avoiding all of the problems just noted.

Nevertheless, pupil-teacher planning is a tremendously valuable school experience and a legitimate part of curriculum design. Where the difficulties described above can be overcome, it should be more commonly used. De Francesco comments on the value and need for this type of planning:

> In a democratic society, preplanned, predigested, and preconceived programs are antagonistic to wholehearted personal or group participation. On the other hand, cooperative planning, digesting, and conceptualization become educative in the highest sense.[19]

In this volume, however, curriculum planning will be viewed within the frame of reference of prior teacher planning, since even the most spontaneous of cooperative plans involve the efforts and judgments of the teacher, in whose hands in our present culture the ultimate authority and responsibility must rest.

The implication in de Francesco's comment, that teacher-pupil planning is related to differentiation of activities on an individual or or small-group basis, is also important to consider. There is, of course, no necessary connection. The art teacher can, logically, assign a range of differentiated projects, even to the extent of a different one to each pupil, chosen by the teacher's estimate of each pupil's needs or interests. However, some measure of consultation with the pupils would seem reasonable and profitable, if only as a means of discovering those needs and interests.

It would appear that most educational theory today recognizes the virtue of an individually differentiated curriculum. The appearance

[19] Italo L. de Francesco, *Art Education, Its Means and Ends* (New York: Harper & Brothers, 1958), p. 361.

Figure 6   *The Cock,* sculpture carved and constructed from pine, mahogany, and metal by a high school student. (Courtesy of Berlin, New Hampshire, Public Schools.)

of the teaching machine on the educational horizon supports this attitude, providing as it does the maximum of individualization. It would be justifiable to assert that, for the most part, art teachers have made use of the individually differentiated curriculum quite as vigorously as teachers in any other secondary subject area. Indeed, it might be said that this type of curriculum approach is probably more common in the art class than in any other high school class, although the reason may well be the practical issue of a lack of concise subject matter to be transmitted in many art courses, rather than the art teacher's theoretical beliefs.

However, there is also little doubt that curriculum design, in the sense of prior planning by teacher or supervisor, must involve some generalization. Even if the secondary art teacher is committed to a different activity for each pupil, some concept of the range of choices must be predetermined. The most striking reason, noted before, is that the art teacher is obligated to some extent to predict the supplies and equipment needed. Rarely is the high school art room so comprehensively stocked that almost any activity can be chosen and carried out by the pupils from materials on hand. Furthermore, it is reasonable to assume that under normal circumstances the art teacher is not well enough acquainted with his pupils to be able to predetermine their needs and interests. At best, this kind of knowledge grows out of the working situation and demands that the art teacher build the greatest degree of flexibility into his curriculum.

Finally, it is of more than passing importance to indicate the possible relevance of some of the newer instructional approaches to secondary art education. Although the three experimental techniques which we will discuss are, perhaps, more properly methodological rather than curricular, the format of this volume strongly suggests their description in this chapter.

The first technique is that of teaching by television. With the growth of this new visual medium, the time-honored audio-visual aids, such as slides, filmstrips, and films, are now supported by an almost limitless instrumentation to bring pictures of art objects, the artists themselves speaking or working, or the activities of other students directly into the art classrooms. Whether the device used is open- or closed-circuit television, in black and white or color, the potential in its use as a classroom aid to the art teacher contains many obviously exciting possibilities. It is therefore most unfortunate that no extensive experimentation with television in secondary art has been maintained. While many communities have had fine arts programs for public viewing, and some school districts have presented programs on art directed towards pupils in the classroom, the most elaborate TV teaching project, the Hagerstown experiment, did not include the visual arts in its roster of curriculum areas.[20]

---

[20] Ford Foundation, *Teaching By Television* (New York, 1961), p. 47.

Figure 7   An eleventh grade pupil carving a wood sculpture. (Courtesy of University School, Florida State University.)

The second technique is that of team teaching, which has been loosely associated with television teaching in its development. Essentially, team teaching has been a staple device in art education, with the traveling art supervisor on the elementary level and the visiting artist on both levels. What this device can offer to the secondary art teacher is the opportunity to include in one course experience the strong points in background and preparation of more than one individual teacher. A seventh-grade art class organized on a team basis might provide a unit on ceramics taught by an expert potter or a series of graphics projects directed by a practicing print maker. Or, conceivably, an art appreciation class could make use of teachers of music and literature in order to coordinate the pupils' insight into the function and development of the arts in our culture.

Needless to say, there has been little sustained experimentation in team teaching in secondary art situations. It would seem that problems of expense, difficulties of scheduling, and above all, the general indifference of educational authorities to art education, have effectively dampened the progressive ardor of the secondary art teacher.

The third experimental technique, that of the teaching machine, is easily but not correctly neglected in its relationship to art education. There seems little doubt that a subjective area such as art can find little use for programed learning with mechanical or electrical apparatus, since teaching machines are presently purely cognitive in function. On the other hand, the visual arts do command a considerable body of factual material, with respect to nomenclature of materials, historical data about art objects and artists, and, possibly, verbal description of particular skill processes or even alternative solutions to particular visual problems.

It therefore does not seem at all farfetched to predict that the secondary art teacher will at some future date make use of the teaching machine in much the same way as the social studies teacher, if the future educational structure is as heavily weighted with technology as present trends suggest.

II

What is Art Education?

The term "art education" as a subject designation properly refers to the teaching of the visual arts. As a segment of the curriculum on every level of education from pre-school activities to graduate studies, art is supported as a worth-while subject in that 1) it is an intrinsically valuable experience, 2) it is an important part of our human and Western culture, and 3) it provides significant contributions to the development of the individual.

Only in its narrowest sense should art education mean the transmittal of a body of factual material or the inculcation of specific media skills. Broadly and properly conceived, this professional area, acting as an integral portion of the total social instrument of education, should be concerned with the maturation and refinement of people. In this vast effort, both historical and technical information and the development of manipulative competencies have their places. However, the emphasis must lie on total human growth.

The historical development of art education supports its consideration as a distinct and sovereign discipline with a reasonably sophisticated philosophy and a well-defined practice in the schools. Although both

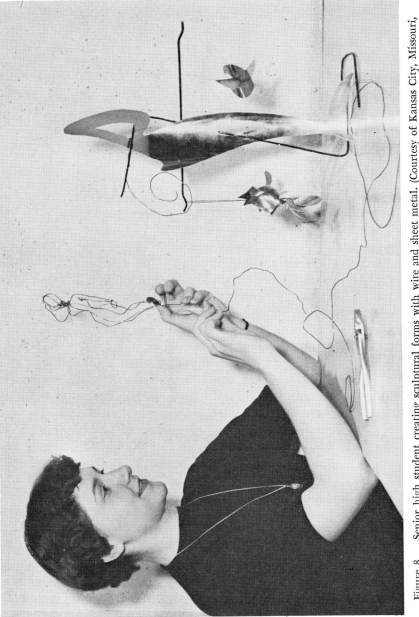

Figure 8   Senior high student creating sculptural forms with wire and sheet metal. (Courtesy of Kansas City, Missouri, Public Schools.)

theory and practice are presently based primarily on authoritative opinions, rather than on scientifically organized empirical evidence, this same basis can be said to be substantially true of all education. There is less research in art education than in, for example, the teaching of reading, but the difference in reliable information is not significant. Indeed, the amount of research in the area of art education is expanding rapidly, and it can be hoped that we will eventually accumulate sufficient reliable knowledge to evaluate our policies on other than authoritative criteria.

Inside the school, art education operates as one of a number of subjects, primarily optional for secondary pupils. The only point at which art is frequently a required experience is on the junior high school level. Therefore, it is reasonable to assume that the visual arts are still seen as a peripheral discipline in our culture, useful as leisure-time activities and as a small segment of the desirable polish of the middle and upper classes, but not germane to the vital task of developing a mature and intelligent citizenry.

Reasons for this unfortunate status of art education are not difficult to discover. Of prime importance is the present role of art and the artist in our society, pungently described in a recent article:

> The fact that we are preoccupied exclusively with commerce, technology and war reduces the artist to two alternative roles. First, he can be society's paid entertainer. If he elects that role, he comes to look upon society as a tired-businessman-at-large, requiring to be amused and distracted so that he may return with renewed vigor to his real interests. Or, if the artist happens not to be good at parlor tricks, or is not in sympathy with tired businessmen, he can retreat into solipsism, write unintelligibly, paint nightmares and otherwise wear a badge of disaffection. There is almost no middle ground between these two choices; it is hardly conceivable that a man of authentic genius in our day can find himself fully in accord with the purposes of our society, and dedicate his art to articulating and celebrating those purposes—the formula for Greek drama, or great art anywhere. In order to have great novels rather than denatured ones, we should have to transform ourselves into a society capable of evoking assent from its brightest spirits.[1]

One might suggest at this point that this is a generalized comment about the arts and not necessarily relevant to art education. However, a similar diagnosis—though stated with less bitterness—can be found in Logan's classic history of the field. "Art education now is in a state of

[1] Emile Capouya, "Native Talent and Trade Practice," *The Nation*, Vol. 191, No. 10 (October 1, 1960), p. 211.

Figure 9   Figure drawing, ink with a watercolor wash, by a twelfth grade pupil.
(Courtesy of Pasadena, California, City Schools.)

bewildering contrasts. Never has so much been written and said about the arts; conversely, never in history have the arts been counted so negligible among the forces that supposedly shape or direct society."[2]

Another reason is the confused and divided opinions of those who speak for art education. While all of us claim to "know" that art is central rather than peripheral to the process of education, we are hard put to agree among ourselves as to why this is so. Our reasons range from the revelation of internal individual truth[3] and the inculcation of transcendental moral principles[4] to nonverbal training for the communication of new scientific concepts[5] and the promotion of international understanding.[6] It is difficult to avoid the suspicion that both theoreticians and practitioners in art education are completely bewildered as to the educational function of their own discipline.

This condition can hardly incite sympathy and support on the part of administrators, supervisors, and the lay public, particularly in the context of contemporary mass ignorance of and disdain for the arts.

Nonetheless, there does exist a well-defined and structured body of theory in art education which has developed with increasing momentum over the last one hundred years. To understand our present position, it is necessary to outline briefly the history of ideas and events in the field. Curricula, like other practical activities, grow from ideas and, therefore, it is the development of ideas that must be stressed in any historical consideration.

HISTORICAL DEVELOPMENTS

> The teaching of art in America has suffered from a variety of misconceptions. It has been thought of as manual discipline, as a genteel accomplishment, as "busy work," and as a safety valve for little savages.[7]

The history of art education in the United States maintains an undisturbed duality of purpose, that is, the development of technical

[2] Frederick Logan, *Growth of Art in American Schools* (New York: Harper & Brothers, 1955), p. 201.

[3] John Lembach, "Art and Science—A Challenge to Art Education," *Art Education, J. of NAEA*, Vol. 14, No. 1 (January, 1961), p. 8.

[4] Herbert Read, *Culture and Education in World Order* (New York: The Museum of Modern Art, 1948), pp. 11, 12.

[5] Lawrence K. Frank, "Role of the Arts in Education," *Studies in Art Education, J. of NAEA*, Vol. 1, No. 2 (Spring, 1960), pp. 28, 29.

[6] Oliver J. Caldwell, "Art and Communication," *Art Education, J. of NAEA*, Vol. 13, No. 8 (November, 1960), p. 4.

[7] Robert Iglehart, *Art Education Today* (New York: Teachers College, Columbia University, 1941), p. 9.

skill and the growth of respect for art tradition, from colonial days almost to the end of the nineteenth century. From the time of Benjamin Franklin, who suggested the possibility of art as a part of the school program as early as 1749 in his "Proposed Hints for an Academy," art education remained the province of the talented or the well-to-do.

Thomas Jefferson, toward the close of the eighteenth century, suggested that young Americans study architecture, since painting and sculpture are "too expensive for the state of wealth among us. They are worth seeing but not studying."[8] Counts comments on this statement: "Not until the frontier was closed and the continent more or less settled could Americans be expected to devote themselves to the refinement of life."[9] Counts feels that political sovereignty and economic expansion were among the prime factors that caused the long delay in the large scale study and practice of art in the United States of that period.

Farnum, in the Fortieth Yearbook of the National Society for the Study of Education, describes this early phase of American art education:

> . . . we find drawing taught as a special and somewhat detached subject, advertised in local newspapers on the one hand by professional painters, who offered such instruction in limited classes with a definite vocational intent, and on the other hand by the boarding-school mistress, who "respectfully solicits a share of the public patronage" for such "ornamental branches" as "Drawing, Embroidery, Music, and making a great variety of fancy articles."[10]

D'Amico sees these two emphases of technical, vocational training and cultural dabbling of the "dilettante" as constant throughout art education history regardless of shifts in philosophy or method in the past century.[11]

The academic tradition of vocational training, brought into the new continent from Europe, concerned itself with technical proficiency and respect for the art of the past and was taught by authoritarian methods and the imitation of the work of old masters. The

[8] George S. Counts, *The Social Foundations of Education* (New York: Charles Scribner's Sons, 1934), p. 349.

[9] *Ibid.*

[10] Royal B. Farnum, "The Early History of American Art Education," *Art in American Life and Education,* Fortieth Yearbook, National Society for the Study of Education (Bloomington, Ill.: Public School Publishing Company, 1941), p. 445.

[11] Victor D'Amico, *The Visual Arts in General Education,* Commission on Secondary School Curriculum, Progressive Education Association (New York: D. Appleton-Century Co., 1940).

cultural education of the middle class worked toward similar goals, seen rather as genteel accomplishments.

The first public educational use of art activities in the curriculum was brought about by William Bentley Fowle in Boston in 1821. Whitford, in describing this period of development in art education, says, "The work was restricted to the teaching of outline drawing, chiefly geometric, by the copy method."[12]

Monroe describes the period 1821-1850 as the era of visual training, where the function and value of art activities were limited to the discipline of perception, eyes, and hands.[13]

In 1848, William Minife of Baltimore advocated the idea of art education in the public schools on the basis of its use in the development of good taste in pupils and for its value in providing evidence of talent which could be trained for the growing industrial power of the nation. At the same time, in Massachusetts, a group of educators were supporting the idea of the use of art in the curriculum of the schools of that state. Through the efforts of these men, Horace Mann, the secretary of the Board of Education in Massachusetts in 1843; John Dudley Philbrick, the superintendent of schools in Boston; and William Newton Bartholomew; the idealogical groundwork was prepared for the appearance of public art education on an appreciable scale in that part of the United States.

Farnum notes the influence of industrial interests in this advent of public art education.

> In the middle of the nineteenth century, a group of industrialists in Massachusetts came to the conclusion that skill in drawing and a knowledge of historic forms of ornament were essential to their manufacture and later, in 1870, an act of the state legislature was passed permitting drawing ("industrial and mechanical") to be "freely" taught in any city and town, and making "free" instruction compulsory in cities and towns of over 10,000 inhabitants.[14]

As a result of this activity, Walter Smith was made director of art for all the public schools of Massachusetts in 1871, and consequently became the first director of art in the United States. Art, or rather "drawing," finally achieved an official place in the curriculum of the

[12] William G. Whitford, *An Introduction to Art Education* (New York: D. Appleton-Century Co., 1937), p. 8.

[13] William S. Monroe, *Encyclopedia of Educational Research* (New York: The Macmillan Company, 1950), p. 64.

[14] Farnum, *op. cit.*, p. 446.

Figure 10   Wire and wood sculptures by junior high school students. (Courtesy
of Long Beach, California, City Schools.)

schools of one of the states, for the purpose of developing industrial
goods which might successfully compete with foreign products.

Monroe designates the period 1851-1870 as that period in which
art education was used to train technical designers. However, it is during this era that statements are found in the very meager literature
on the subject containing conceptions of art as something more than
vocational preparation, a genteel accomplishment, or a means for the
selection of industrial designers. Whitford quotes a report of that
period:

> Art education, even for little children, means something more
> than instruction in drawing. It comprehends the cultivation of the
> eye, that it may perceive form; of the hand, that it may represent
> form graphically (drawing); of the mind, that it may receive and
> express ideas in regard to form.[15]

[15] Whitford, *op. cit.*, p. 64.

Exercise books based on these ideas, one for each elementary grade, consisted of a series of drawings on one page with a blank page opposite on which the drawing was to be copied.

Another later report, almost contemporary in its flavor to Whitford, states that, ". . . the instruction is to be varied and rational, the aim being not to make proficients in any one thing, but to impart a taste, a knowledge, and a skill of universal utility."[16] It must be noted that these are isolated statements and, further, that there is no record of their implementation in the classroom.

In the period 1871-1900 emphasis shifted from practical objectives to a cultural purpose. Stimulated by public school art exhibits at national expositions such as the Philadelphia Centennial Exposition in 1876 and the World's Columbian Exposition at Chicago in 1893, art education began to become more popular in the schools.

This increase in the interest shown in art education and the changes in emphasis of the thought of that time are exemplified by the formation of a Committee on Drawing by the National Education Association. A report of this group published in 1899 states the aims of art education as the following:

1. To offer a consistent development of the faculty of sight.
2. To develop an appreciation of the beautiful.
3. To acquire ability to represent (objects).
4. To develop the creative impulse.
5. To prepare pupils for manual industry is purely incidental.
6. The development of professional artists is in no sense the aim of art in education in the public schools.[17]

Individual educators also exerted influence on this shifting of values in art education. A figure of such stature at the turn of the century was Arthur Wesley Dow. He claimed that, "a better understanding of the true usefulness of art recognizes creative power as a divine gift, the natural endowment of every human soul, showing itself at first in the form that we call appreciation."[18] Dow felt that this appreciation motivated some people to create works of art and most people to desire more beauty in their environment. Therefore, schools should "educate

[16] *Ibid.* (quoted from "Records and Awards," *Report of the U. S. Centennial Commission,* Vol. 8, 1876, p. 28).

[17] Walter Klar, Leon L. Winslow, and C. Valentine Kirby, *Art Education in Principle and Practice* (Springfield, Mass.: Milton Bradley Company, 1933), p. 27.

[18] Arthur Wesley Dow, *Theory and Practice of Teaching Art* (New York: Teachers College, Columbia University, 1908), p. 55.

Figure 11   Tempera painting, senior high school. (Courtesy of Pasadena, California, City Schools.)

the whole people for appreciation." Dow also advocated practice in design or composition as a means of developing this appreciation.[19]

Another writer with a similar preoccupation, Ross, ". . . is driven by the desire to classify and codify the slightest movement of the pencil."[20] The same motivation of organizing design principles for more effective teaching was carried into the twenties, by Hambridge and Best-Maugard.

Nevertheless, the large scale emphasis in public school art remained, during these years, centered on the academic tradition of technical proficiency and veneration for the old masters, though the old formulae of copying and cast drawing began to be replaced by exercises in "design." As with most new ideas, social institutions were slow to embrace innovations in thought. Moreover, the impressionist movement in painting with its "scientific" orientation, which became increasingly better known in the first decade of the twentieth century, pointed toward the same development of technique acquired via the formula. Also, as D'Amico states,

> . . . the dominant theory in general education was Herbartianism, with its "five formal steps." The term *formal* indicated that here was a formula applicable to all teaching situations. In art, too, emphasis was laid on design principles, on color theory, and on laws of perspective drawing.[21]

Color charts, value scales, and decorative borders became standard methods with which to inculcate principles of design, and ultimately, the appreciation of beauty.

Another line of development that exerted pressure on the public schools of that era was the growth of the idea of manual training or industrial arts. Work in the manual arts was given in American schools as early as 1866, and continued under different names as an important part of the school program. The goals of the industrial arts program were seen as practical experience with tools and the satisfaction derived from constructive activities. The area was almost exclusively limited to boys.

De Francesco suggests that the industrial arts program was aided in its growth by the International Art Congress at Dresden in 1897 which

---

[19] Arthur Wesley Dow, *Composition* (Garden City, N.Y.: Doubleday Page and Company, 1918).

[20] Denman Ross, *The Theory of Pure Design* (Boston: Houghton Mifflin Company, 1907).

[21] D'Amico, *op. cit.*, p. 5.

Figure 12   Mixed media: conté crayon and tempera drawing and painting by a
high school senior. (Courtesy of Pasadena, California, City Schools.)

". . . made America conscious of the fact that even in our public schools art must take cognizance of the following needs: 1) better designed products, 2) greater color discrimination, and 3) discovery of talent for further training."[22] It would seem that the only new concept encountered here is the stress on color.

Eventually, industrial arts became an area of study and practice apart from art education, but at that time, there was as yet no clear distinction. Theory in both fields occupied a common ground. At the present time, of course, industrial arts is a distinctively separate field in American schools.

Between the years 1901 and 1920, the child-centered movement in early childhood and elementary education began to influence art educational thought. At the same time, Expressionism in painting grew in popularity among artists and art teachers. Concepts such as creative self-expression and originality began to appear in art education terminology. By the early 1920's, mainly through the international influence of Franz Cizek and two other Viennese art teachers, Rothe and Thetter, art education theory in the United States caught up the slogan of freedom in art expression. In Cizek's own words, "Great creative energy exists in every child. This must find an outlet in expression or repression will result. Children should be allowed to draw what they wish, what they see in their mind's eye, not that which others think they ought to draw."[23] In America, this approach to art experiences was advocated by Hughes Mearns, and an exposition of its philosophy can be found in his writings and those of Hartman and Schumaker.[24]

An example of the type of thought on the subject of creativity advocated by this group can be seen in an article by Mearns. He says:

> He [the child] needs little or no instruction, but he must have materials and his surroundings must be such as to call his effort worthy; he is susceptible to condemnation and he will give up all his precious art and lose one of the most gracious of nature's gifts if his overlords command.[25]

[22] Italo L. de Francesco, *An Evaluation of Curricula for the Preparation of Teachers of Art.* Unpublished doctoral dissertation, New York University, 1943.

[23] Wilhelm Viola, *Child Art and Franz Cizek* (New York: The John Day Company, Inc., 1936), p. 6.

[24] Hughes Mearns, *Creative Youth* (Garden City, N.Y.: Doubleday Page and Company, 1925); Gertrude Hartman and Ann Schumaker, *Creative Expression* (New York: The John Day Company, Inc., 1932).

[25] Hughes Mearns, "The Creative Spirit and Its Significance to Education," *Progressive Education*, Vol. 3 (April-May-June, 1926), p. 101.

D'Amico evaluates the contribution of this viewpoint with the following statement:

> The doctrine of self-expression had one outstanding and important value. It recognized the child as an individual and focused interest upon him, while the academic and formal viewpoints either denied the child or regretted his immaturity. In this respect it paved the way for learning much about child behavior and creativity.[26]

These lines of thought in education and art education finally culminated in a considerable professional acceptance of the significance of art education.

An important date in art education history, is the 1927 meeting of the National Education Association in Dallas, Texas. It was then that, for the first time, art education was given general recognition as a fundamental in the curriculum of public education.

Two specific incidents helped to bring about this acceptance. The Department of Superintendence of the National Education Association in 1925 attempted to outline goals for art education, and McAndrew in the report of that body stressed these values in art activities: 1) appreciation of beauty in art and nature, 2) initiative and originality, and 3) creation of a more beautiful environment. Also in 1925, the Federated Council on Art Education conceived the purposes of elementary school art as: 1) appreciation, 2) skills, 3) knowledge, 4) habits, attitudes, and ideals, and 5) growth of outstanding abilities.

In the thirties, the operation of a University of Minnesota sponsored community project in art education attracted considerable attention and helped to develop a broadening scope of art activities in the schools. Based on the ideas of Haggerty and others, the Owatonna project had a simple but vital philosophy which was emulated on varying scales in other communities. These ideas are summarized as: 1) no differentiation is made between useful and fine arts, 2) art is viewed as relating to every aspect of living, and 3) the devolopment of skills, though an integral part of the program, is secondary to the pupil's growth in aesthetic discrimination as it affects everyday living.[27]

The decade of the thirties brought still another aspect of value in art activities to the attention of American education. This concept,

---

[26] D'Amico, *op. cit.,* p. 7.

[27] Donald Laging, *Art Education Today,* (New York: Teachers College, Columbia University, 1942), p. 57.

Figure 13   Photography as a medium in the visual arts in high school.
(Courtesy of Los Angeles, California, Public Schools.)

with historical precedent in the writings of John Ruskin and William Morris, considered one function of art as the training of the individual for the present and future reorganization of his environment on a more aesthetic basis. A volume on curriculum construction published in 1936 expresses the growth of this idea. "Since 1925 the development of good taste and discrimination, both in the selection of personal items and in creating beauty in one's environment, has become a major objective."[28] Also suggestive of this viewpoint is the title of one of the sections of the chapter on art in the same volume, "Building a More Beautiful America Through Art Education." An important theoretical basis upon which this concept was constructed was the idea that aesthetic value can and should be derived from many aspects of everyday living. Supported by Mearns and others of that school of thought, this concept received considerable impetus in the writings of Melvin Haggerty,[29] and later, from the experimental Owatonna Art Education Project.[30]

Due also to an increase of social awareness on the part of educators and artists in the period following the economic collapse of 1929, the idea was aided by the critical writings of such men as Mumford, Bel Geddes, and Frankl. Even today, it remains an integral part of the theoretical picture of values in art, and can be discovered among the lists of aims in many courses of study.[31]

By 1940, these several interpretations of value in art formed the ideological basis of formulations of aims. Several studies survey the picture of objectives believed important at the time. Hilpert, writing in 1941, sees six major trends in value operating in the area of art education: 1) the theory of "Art for Art's Sake," stressing art as a product with intrinsic and unique value, 2) appreciation, picture study or factual, historical concentration, 3) creative self-expression, supporting ". . . immediate experiences of actual manipulation of some art medium," 4) correlation of art with some other curricular area, 5) art as a part of the integrated curriculum, and 6) art activities stressing manual or industrial arts.[32]

A report of the American Council on Education recommended that extensive experimentation be done to determine the role of the arts

[28] John J. Norton and Margaret A. Norton, *Foundations of Curriculum Building* (Boston: Ginn and Company, 1936), p. 467.

[29] Melvin E. Haggerty, *Art, A Way of Life* (Minneapolis, Minn.: University of Minnesota Press, 1944).

[30] Edwin Ziegfeld and Mary E. Smith, *Art for Daily Living: The Story of the Owatonna Art Education Project* (Minneapolis, Minn.: University of Minnesota Press, 1944).

[31] An example of this viewpoint discussed as early as 1929 can be found in Fredrik V. Nyquist, *Art Education in Elementary Schools* (Baltimore, Md.: Warwick & York, Inc., 1929), pp. 21, 22.

[32] Robert S. Hilpert, "Changing Emphases in School Art Programs," *Art in American Life and Education,* Fortieth Yearbook, National Society for the Study of Education (Bloomington, Ill.: Public School Publishing Company, 1941), pp. 448-452.

in secondary schools. The experiments should deal with the following phases of the art program:

1. The role of the arts in helping children to understand and appreciate the culture of other groups and epochs, for the children ". . . must accept the validity of the experience of nations and cultures other than their own and must learn to respect them."

2. The role of the aesthetic arts as a means of expression of personal experience. Adolescents especially seem to need opportunities for self-expression as they are seeking to state and verify their life objectives. "A development of skill in the arts would then increase the adolescents' opportunities to be themselves."

3. The use of aesthetic expression as a means of relaxing emotional tensions and restoring morale.

4. The examining of young peoples' art products in order to understand better their conflicts and needs through an understanding of their "fantasy life."[33]

In 1940, D'Amico saw the broad general aim of education in the secondary school ". . . is to further the growth of individuals in rich enjoyment and effectiveness and to encourage them to create a society where such living is possible for all."[34]

Reviewing recent trends in 1943, de Francesco discussed purposes of art education.

> While even the most recent statements do not show total agreement, there are many common denominators in all of them. These seem to be:
>
> a. Appreciation and taste for all.
> b. Art is related to areas of life activities.
> c. Dicovery and cultivation of talent for productive art fields.
> d. Expression as a means of education.
> e. Experience as way [sic] to art understanding and personal growth.[35]

The National Commission on Cooperative Curriculum Planning reported the values of art activities in 1941 in the following areas: 1) art in personal living, 2) art in the home environment, 3) art in the

---

[33] Daniel Prescott, ed., *Emotion and the Educative Process* (Washington, D.C.: American Council on Education, 1938), pp. 224-227.

[34] D'Amico, *op. cit.*, pp. 17, 18.

[35] de Francesco, *op. cit.*, p. 68.

Figure 14 *Street Scene*, a watercolor painting by a twelfth grade pupil. (Courtesy of Honolulu Academy of Arts, Honolulu, Hawaii)

community, 4) art in consumer selection, 5) art in appreciation, 6) art in expression.[36]

CURRENT CONCEPTS

The decade of the forties saw a rapid growth of publications in art education. In addition to Ziegfeld, D'Amico, and de Francesco, authors such as Schaefer-Simmern, Lowenfeld, and Read, produced writings which broadened and filled in the framework of conceptualizations in art education. This decade saw a particular emphasis on patterns of child development in art. In this area the last three men wrote prolifically. Perhaps the classic statement about child growth in art is Viktor Lowenfeld's *Creative and Mental Growth,* published in 1947.

A wealth of new ideas and new emphases burgeoned within the field, promoting an ever-widening interest in and respect for the role of the visual arts in human growth. Ideas such as the need and value of "creative expression," inherited from earlier years, were more clearly articulated and more fully documented. Timmins writes:

> The continuous and dynamic process which is creative expression exists in the very nerve cells of the human organism and is basic to all education and learning. It is the fundamental fact which makes necessary the education of the individual in all the expressive inventive activities by which he discovers himself and his relation to the world.[37]

Another description of the creative process states that:

> Ability to create by means of visual forms is a natural attribute of man. It grows and unfolds in a natural way; it moves from simple visual concepts to more complicated schema until it reaches the fullest development to a degree determined and limited only by the child's biological and psychological endowment.[38]

Even standard texts and reports in general education paid heed to the concepts and terminology of art education.[39]

[36] John DeBoer, *The Subject Fields in General Education* (New York: D. Appleton-Century Company, 1941), pp. 187-204.

[37] James Timmins, "Some Basic Human Needs of the Individual," *This is Art Education,* Yearbook of the NAEA, 1951, p. 32.

[38] Italo de Francesco, "Experience as Basis for Creative Growth," *This is Art Education,* Yearbook of the NAEA, 1952, p. 131.

[39] *What the High School Ought to Teach* (Washington, D.C.: American Youth Commission, 1940), pp. 30, 31; Arthur Jersild, *Child Development and the Curriculum* (New York: Teachers College, Columbia University, 1946), p. 89.

The idea of promoting mental hygiene through art activities received widespread recognition and endorsement in this decade. Although mentioned as early as Aristotle,[40] and clearly described by writers such as Dewey, Frank, Zachry, and Edman[41] in the late twenties and early thirties, the idea became a major concept in this decade. In 1946, Giles wrote:

> One of the benefits which has been stressed in recent years is the therapeutic release of feelings gained by pounding clay, metal, wood or by solving problems of construction, or by feeling a sense of achievement that comes when something in beautiful color has been made.[42]

In a careful analysis of the relationship of psychology and art, the authors state that, ". . . children turn towards creative media to express feelings, concerns, and anxieties which ordinarily are not permissible in more overt form . . ."[43]

Along with the conception of art as therapy comes the idea of art as a diagnostic medium. Lowenfeld writes that, "What the child draws is his subjective experience of what is important to him during the act of drawing . . . the drawing gives us an excellent record of the things which are of special mental or emotional importance to the child."[44]

Another facet of the role of art in education popularized in the literature of this period was the idea of art experiences promoting the integration of the personality. Dewey noted that, ". . . the process (of art production) entails the integrated functioning of emotion, imagination, and intelligence, in re-ordering the environment."[45] Cane claims that, "Art may be a means of activating all one's functions; the simultaneous use of these functions assists in the integration of the personality."[46] She continues by explaining that:

[40] Aristotle, *Politics,* trans. by H. Rackham (Cambridge, Mass.: Harvard University Press, 1950), p. 657.

[41] John Dewey, *Art as Experience* (New York: Minton, Balch & Company, 1934), pp. 77, 78; Caroline B. Zachry, *Art Education Today* (New York: Teachers College, Columbia University, 1937), p. 42; and Irwin Edman, *Arts and the Man* (New York: W. W. Norton & Company, Inc., 1928), p. 17.

[42] Harold H. Giles, "Arts and the Democratic Ideal," *Arts in Childhood* (New York: Association for Arts in Childhood, 1946), Series 2, No. 1, p. 23.

[43] Rose H. Alschuler and LaBerta W. Hattwick, *Painting and Personality* (Chicago: University of Chicago Press, 1947), p. 161.

[44] Viktor Lowenfeld, *Creative and Mental Growth* (New York: The Macmillan Company, 1947), p. 62.

[45] Dewey, *op. cit.,* p. 31.

[46] Florence Cane, *The Artist in Each of Us* (New York: Pantheon Books, Inc., 1951), p. 33.

Figure 15   Stage set and costumes designed and executed by high school students for the play "The Admirable Crichton." (Courtesy of Kansas City, Missouri, Public Schools.)

There is a correspondence between these functions of the human being and the underlying principles of art. The function of movement is related to the principle of rhythm; feeling to dynamics and harmony; and thought, balance. Since the principles of art correspond to human functions, one may therefore gradually integrate functions through the practice of art. By this fortunate relation, the teaching of art can be a valuable method for the growth and integration of the individual.[47]

By 1950, the professional area of art education was firmly established, though on a relatively minor scale, in the curriculum of the public schools. The development of the National Art Education Association and Committee on Art Education of the Museum of Modern Art gives further evidence of professional strength and self-identification. The publication of the NAEA yearbooks, starting in 1951, stimulated the production of a mass of sometimes scholarly and often readable material. Numbers of books and articles were published in the field and numberless speeches were given at conferences.

Despite this energetic activity, however, no new ideas of any consequence emerged during this decade. The two prime issues of the period were (and still are in the sixties) the development of creativity and the concept of the artist-teacher. Initiated by the researches of J. P. Guilford at the University of Southern California[48] and Lowenfeld at Pennsylvania State University,[49] and provoked by the political and technological competition between the United States and the Soviet Union, the concept of growth in creativity was eagerly embraced by almost all art educators. In fact, this rivalry, punctuated by a series of Soviet successes in space exploration, turned the attention of the nation through its mass media of communication toward public education and, more particularly, toward academic training. This trend caused some erosion of the advances in status that art education had won for itself, and produced an almost exaggerated absorption with the capacity of art experiences to engender creative capabilities and attitudes, culminating in the hypothesis that creativity in art can "transfer" to other areas of human action.[50] In fact Hoffa, writing about creativity in a recent publication, claims:

> The assumption of a transfer of the effects of art experience to other phases of human behavior is unquestionably the most basic tenet of art education, and it is because of the almost universal

[47] *Ibid.*, p. 34.

[48] J. P. Guilford, "Can Creativity Be Developed?" *Art Education, J. of NAEA,* Vol. 11, No. 6 (June, 1958), pp. 3-18.

[49] Viktor Lowenfeld, "The Adolescence of Art Education," *Art Education, J. of NAEA,* Vol. 10, No. 7, (October, 1957), pp. 5-12.

[50] Viktor Lowenfeld and Kenneth R. Beittel, "Interdisciplinary Criteria in the Arts and Sciences: A Progress Report," *Research in Art Education,* Ninth Yearbook of the NAEA, 1959, pp. 35-44; and Kenneth R. Beittel (ed.), *Art Education Bulletin, Eastern Arts Association Research Bulletin,* Vol. 18, No. 4 (April, 1961), pp. 66-72.

acceptance of its validity that art education has emerged as a separate academic discipline.[51]

Further studies in the area of creativity in art education are presently being spearheaded by Beittel and his associates at Pennsylvania State University, McFee at Stanford University, and Barkan and Hausman at Ohio State University. Studies of creativity in other disciplines are being made by Paul Torrance at the University of Minnesota, Calvin Taylor and Brewster Ghiselin at the University of Utah, and Frank Barron at the University of California at Berkeley. While a wide range of descriptive (and some possibly predictive) factors have been isolated by these studies, most researchers caution that there is no sound basis for structuring changes in classroom teaching on present research findings. These investigations can be properly considered as exploratory, as providing the raw material out of which new significant hypotheses may be generated.

The concept of the artist-teacher, while not yet one of general significance, illustrates a growing tendency in the field to return to our original historical preoccupation with aesthetic concerns. The idea is stated simply by McCracken:

> . . . there are indications that high level artisitic activity is essential to an understanding and appreciation of the full dimensions of aesthetic experience as they relate to educational processes.[52]

Further embellishments are contributed by Conant:

> I would like to comment briefly on the concept of the art teacher as an artist-scholar-teacher. . . . While he may not have as much time to spend on art production as most professional artists, he realizes that personal and reasonably significant production in at least one art medium is essential to his understanding and proper encouragement of the creative process in others.[53]

An alternative viewpoint is expressed by Logan and Lanier.[54] Logan writes:

> The end result of setting up the goals of the artist as applicable both to artist and teacher is to make less effectual the work of many

[51] Harlan E. Hoffa, *Art Education Bulletin, Eastern Arts Association Research Bulletin,* Vol. 18, No. 4 (April, 1961), p. 66.

[52] Willard McCracken, "Artist-Teacher," *Art Education, J. of NAEA,* Vol. 12, No. 9 (December, 1959), p. 5.

[53] Howard Conant, "The Role of the Arts in Education, Part 11," *Art Education Bulletin, Eastern Arts Association Research Bulletin,* Vol. 17, No. 6 (September, 1960), pp. 9, 10.

[54] Vincent Lanier, "Affectation and Art Education," *Art Education, J. of NAEA,* Vol. 12, No. 7 (October, 1959), pp. 10, 21.

teachers who have, through this process, come to lack pride in their teaching achievement.[55]

Related to the trend of thought that the practice of art provides some special insights requisite to the effective teaching of art, is the presently severely limited extreme view that art education should be

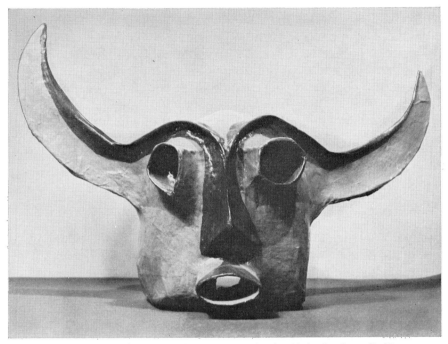

Figure 16   Papier-mâché mask created by a junior high school pupil. (Courtesy of Long Beach, California, City Schools.)

confined to the development of high level skills and knowledges in and about the fine arts. Manzella,[56] in a vituperative paperback, exploits this position, suggesting, in effect, that there is no merit to art education as a separate area and calling for a return to a "solids" teaching of art reminiscent of the basic education enthusiasts.

One final consideration in this brief survey of ideas is the assertion that productive activity in art involves intellectual growth, the develop-

[55] Frederick M. Logan, "Artist in the Schoolroom: A Modern Dilemma," *Studies in Art Education, J. of NAEA*, Vol. 2, No. 2 (Spring, 1961), p. 68.

[56] David Manzella, *Educationists and the Evisceration of the Visual Arts* (Scranton, Pa.: International Textbook Company, 1963).

ment of problem-solving ability in one phase or mode of intelligence. This function of art education, one of long historical standing in the field, has a theoretical basis in Dewey, who said:

> Any idea that ignores the necessary role of intelligence in production of works of art is based upon identification of thinking with use of one special kind of material, verbal signs and words. To think effectively in terms of relations of qualities is as severe a demand upon thought as to think in terms of symbols, verbal and mathematical.[57]

In recent years, the same idea has been given an empirically substantiated footing in the work of Guilford:

> One kind (of intelligence) may be called CONCRETE intelligence because the material dealt with is in the form of things that you can see or hear or feel. The objects dealt with may be visual forms with the various properties that visual forms can have or they may be speech sounds or musical sounds, to mention the most common varieties of concrete materials.[58]

The idea in slightly varied forms has been reintroduced into the contemporary periodical literature in an effort to support the educational contribution of art.[59]

In summary, it might be said that art education theory has evolved within the framework organized by the following basic concepts:

1. All children are capable of growth through art experiences, not just the talented few.
2. Art is a quality that is potential in all visual daily human experience and not restricted to "objets d'art" in a museum.
3. Art education is concerned with total human growth and not just with aesthetic development.
4. The most satisfying and inclusive technique for understanding and enjoying art is the doing of it.
5. Creativity can be inculcated or maintained through art experiences.
6. Art experiences promote the development of problem-solving ability, particularly in the visual and plastic modes of activity.

[57] Dewey, *op. cit.*, p. 46.
[58] Guilford, *op. cit.*, p. 7.
[59] David W. Ecker, *The Uniqueness of Art Learning, Western Arts Association Bulletin,* Vol. 45, No. 2 (January, 1961), pp. 17-29; and Vincent Lanier, "Freedom from Fear," *Insight, Journal of the Southern California Art Education Association,* Vol. 1, No. 2 (Spring, 1960), pp. 2, 3; and Nathaniel Champlin and Francis Villemain (eds.), "Dewey and Creative Education," *Saturday Review* (November 21, 1959), pp. 19-26, 52.

7. In the art experience, the total organism can be deeply involved, providing growth on a fully integrated basis.

8. Art experiences can provide both emotional release and the development of self confidence.

While art education cannot presently compete with more substantially situated subjects such as industrial arts, music, and of course, the academic areas, the view of art as a curricular frill is reasonably infrequent among those in supervision and administration. The impact of reactionary educational tendencies caused by international political competition is at best problematical today. Whether we shall indeed lose ground as a frill subject, as some believe, or will maintain or even enlarge our toehold in the curriculum, is a matter for anyone's conjecture. It is abundantly clear, however, that no degree of operational diminution will erase the creditable tradition of theory contained in our literature.[60]

[60] For greater historical detail and different emphases see Italo de Francesco, *Art Education, Its Means and Ends* (New York: Harper and Brothers, 1958), pp. 61-121; Frederick Logan, *Growth of Art in American Schools* (New York: Harper and Brothers, 1955), pp. xiv and 310; John Rios, *The History of Secondary Art Education,* unpublished doctoral dissertation, University of Texas, 1954; a series of five articles by Robert Saunders, "Little Frogs in the Pond," and so forth, *Everyday Art* (Sandusky, Ohio: American Crayon Company), Vol. 35 (Spring, 1957), Vol. 36 (Fall, 1957; Winter, 1957-58; Spring, 1958), and Vol. 37 (Winter, 1958-59); Francis B. Belshe, *A History of Art Education in the Public Schools of the U. S.,* unpublished doctoral dissertation, Yale University, 1946; and Earl A. Weiley, *Socio-Economic Influences in the Development of American Art Education in the Nineteenth Century,* unpublished doctoral dissertation, Michigan State University, 1957.

III

Analyzing
the Environment

The first step in the design of an effective curriculum on any level is to obtain all the data that can be gathered on those for whom the curriculum is being organized. A careful analysis of the pupils and the environment in which they are to be taught must precede any specific planning. There is little doubt that the general objectives in a particular discipline—conceptualizations of values of a general nature to be derived from experiences in that discipline—are brought already formed to the task of curriculum design by the teacher or supervisor. Nonetheless, specific objectives, or the precise art learnings to be planned for, cannot be described without reference to the nature of the group taught.

Inlow suggests that:

> Assuming that all effective teachers make an early determination of educational objectives, course content, learning methods, and classroom procedures, each teacher will conceive them in a frame of reference that differs from situation to situation yet has common features throughout. Planning, whenever employed, is always a function

49

of time, the teacher's background, the constituency of the class, and the facilities and materials of instruction.[1]

It might indeed be safe to insist that except for broadly conceived areas of value, no aspect of a curriculum can be devised without reference to considerations of the individual group in question. Granting this assumption, it is reasonable to propose that a curriculum must re-

Figure 17   Wood, tissue, and yarn construction made in junior high school. (Courtesy of Long Beach, California, City Schools.)

main flexible enough to be reorganized, or even reoriented, as soon as there are significant changes in the nature of the groups being taught or that the teacher must remain willing to adapt the curriculum to changing groups of students. It is not difficult to recognize that this is in fact what most art teachers do, although they may well reject this description of their actions as too "high sounding."

In order to analyze the group and its environment, the teacher will

[1] Gail M. Inlow, *Maturity in High School Teaching* (Englewood Cliffs, N. J.: Prentice-Hall, Inc., 1963), p. 76.

have to turn to sources of information outside his own direct observation. Let us say, for example, that you have been hired as the art teacher for a new high school which has been in operation for only one year. Let us also suppose that you have not lived in the community in which the school is situated and are therefore unfamiliar with the area and its citizens. You might then turn to agencies such as the local government, the Chamber of Commerce, the PTA, and the local newspaper, as well as the school itself, for your information.

Perhaps it would be well to carry our example a bit further. What information should we look for from these various agencies? In order to provide our hypothetical case with reasonable data, let us further suppose that the high school, John Dewey High School, is in a unified school district and in the incorporated township of Las Blusas in Oceanside County, California. In this way, by illustration, our outline will, perhaps, be easier to adapt to the situation which may face the reader.

It is necessary to note initially that, since school districts in California are free to determine the organization of their educational program, the Las Blusas school district follows what is commonly referred to as an 8–4 plan. In this plan children in grades K–8 attend an elementary school, whereas pupils in grades 9–12 go to a four-year high school.

THE COMMUNITY

The first area of investigation should be the residential, commercial, industrial, and recreational environment in which the homes of the children of John Dewey High School are situated, and which share in the formation of the children's general attitudes, specific school responses, and even, to a considerable extent, their range of capabilities. It seems obvious and trite to state that communities differ widely; yet, there is need to emphasize the importance of recognizing and considering the social milieux of the pupils in any scheme of learning experiences.

The first aspect of the community that warrants examination is the *location*. We find that the town of Las Blusas is nestled between the foothills of the Santa Blanca mountains and the ocean. It is almost neatly bisected by U. S. Highway 101, and is, therefore, only thirty-five minutes driving time from downtown Los Angeles. Though there is considerable coastal fog, particularly during the winter, the town has a mild year-round climate, with an average maximum temperature of

72.1F and an average minimum temperature of 51.7F. The average yearly rainfall is twenty-two inches.

The Chamber of Commerce informs us that Las Blusas is approximately sixteen square miles in *size* and that its *population* is 39,540. While, like almost every portion of southern California, it has grown considerably in population during the period after World War II, the growth has not been as phenomenal as that of many other communities. This, one might surmise, is due primarily to the lack of concentration of industry in the area.

The *socioeconomic level* of the community is lower middle-class, with an average yearly income of $6,900. There is no single major occupational group, although many of the townspeople work in the local and nearby light manufacturing plants that seemed to suddenly appear during the 1950's. There are still many farms, a small dairy industry, the usual proportion of fishermen found in any California coastal town, and the requisite number of local merchants. Las Blusas is not a wealthy community, nor is it a poor one. In fact, it aspires to be a typical American town.

The citizens of this community represent several *prevalent cultural patterns*. About 30 per cent are descendants of Spanish and Portugese fishermen and farmers, and in many of these homes the children hear as much of one of these two languages as they do English. The remainder of the population is polyglot in its derivation, with few non-American oriented home situations. There is no single dominant religious group, although the large number of Spanish and Portugese speaking citizens are almost exclusively Roman Catholic.

The *educational attitudes and activities* of the community vary but little from what might be found in any other town of similar size. The schools are supported by a fairly large and active PTA, the elementary school PTA group being more vigorous than that of the high school. The local American Legion post, through its Americanism chairman, has been keeping a watchful eye on the school library, while the Citizen's Advisory Committee on Education for National Survival (Oceanside County branch) has carefully scrutinized the district schools.

It would be fair to say that Las Blusas has a typical public contemporary attitude toward education: superficially interested, but uninformed.

Community art activities consist of a) the local chapter of the Oceanside County Art Association, b) painting classes held two evenings a week at the local art and crafts shop and taught by the senior member of the small artists' colony, and c) a yearly poster contest sponsored by the Merchant's Association, with cash prizes of $25, $10, and $5.

School use of community resources is sporadic and usually confined to the social studies and science programs. Both the small manufacturing plants and the canneries are visited by high school classes in an effort to illustrate the role of industry and technology in American life. The electronics firms, a few being branches of larger organizations, send several speakers a year to the high school science classes, primarily to promote career interest on the part of the more able science students. No use is made of the light but existing art interest in the community, save for the poster contest, which is usually won by a Dewey High senior.

THE SCHOOL PLANT

The second area of investigation is the school plant. The *size* of the school is approximately 26,000 square feet of floor space, situated on 12½ acres of ground. There are eleven separate one-story buildings of red Roman brick façade, in what might be called a contemporary architectural style. The *condition of the buildings* and the *landscaping* is, of course, excellent since it is a brand new school. While the foliage around the buildings is presently sparse and small, it has been carefully chosen and tastefully arranged.

The *arrangement of rooms* is compact and coherent, with one wing devoted to art classes. While the art rooms are situated far enough away from academic classrooms to permit activity noise, they are not at the farthest end of the campus. There is, consequently, no physical basis for any feeling of isolation for the art faculty or students.

The *art rooms* themselves are three in number and there is also a large, easily accessible storeroom at the end of the wing. The rooms are quite large (1,400 sq ft), well lighted, with half-wall windows on one side, fixed clerestory-like windows on the opposite wall, and an adequate number of grid-covered fluorescent lighting fixtures. Ventilation is adequate. The special venetian blinds which have been ordered will make possible the showing of films and slides in sufficient darkness. While the ceramics room has two large stainless steel sinks, the plumbing in the two general art rooms is too small, and is poorly placed. End-of-the-period clean-up time can become a problem, since congestion at the sink will block off one of the doors to the classroom. Display space has been generously provided, with both large tackboard panels on three walls in each room and a locked, glass-enclosed display case in each of the rooms. Storage space, on the other hand, is in short supply. The large common storeroom and the built-in storage cabinets

Figure 18   Exterior view of a contemporary high school building. (Courtesy of
New York City Public Schools.)

in the art rooms adequately house materials and supplies but cannot suffice for anything but the most limited amount of student work in progress. The formica-topped work tables are attractive and efficient but have no storage drawers attached to them.

The per-pupil expense for the high school is $310. There is no *art budget* as such, but as the per-pupil allocation suggests, there is adequate district money, and the history of financial support for art by the school administration has been excellent. Materials are purchased through school requisitions from the one local art store or through Los Angeles firms. Small items or emergency supplies can be obtained directly by the art faculty through the school's "revolving cash fund," a practice which is permitted but not encouraged.

Materials and equipment are, therefore, plentiful. Nonexpendable equipment in the art rooms includes the following:[2]

6 large tables	1 drafting table
1 work table	1 compressor
3 sets of gas and air outlets	2 buffers
2 kilns (one large, one small)	1 enameling kiln
1 slip mixer	1 ball mill
1 sink trap	2 sinks
5 table looms	2 electric potter's wheels
3 large zinc-lined cupboards	6 zinc-lined storage bins for
1 workbench	clay

Individual storage trays for each student

Audio-visual equipment available for use in art classes includes:

6 16mm motion picture projectors with mobile stand and reels
6 Combination 2″ × 2″ slide and filmstrip projectors
1 3¼″ × 4″ projector, overhead or slide, with mobile stand
1 Opaque projector with mobile stand
2 Overhead projectors
6 Tape recorders, dual speed, dual track, classroom model

Although the school library contains a moderately large stock of art books and periodicals, and the county audio-visual library has a reasonable supply of films and filmstrips on art, there is a serious need for additional visual and verbal resource materials of all kinds. The art teachers find that their own personal book, magazine, and slide collections are more often in their classrooms than in their homes.

THE STUDENTS

The third major area of consideration is the student body. The *student body* of John Dewey High School numbers 1,200 students, ranging in age from 14 to 19 years. The average daily attendance is 1,163. The *I. Q. range* is 74 to 143, and the median is 103. The

[2] A comprehensive listing of facilities and materials for the art room can be found in H. Conant and A. Randall, *Art in Education* (Peoria, Ill.: Charles A. Bennett, 1959), pp. 229-275; and in the *Bulletin of the National Association of Secondary School Principals,* Vol. 45, No. 263 (March, 1961), pp. 62-81, which has also been published by the NAEA as a pamphlet entitled *Art in the Secondary School.*

pupil *classroom response* seems good in general. The high school has its quota of problem students and disinterestedness, but the majority of the boys and girls seem alert and attentive in class. A survey of teachers' answers to a question on pupil attitudes toward learning indicates that they rate their pupils as "high" in interest. The boys and girls seem generally well fed, well dressed, and well mannered. The walkways between classroom buildings are noisy, but orderly, during change of classes. Neither the drop-out nor the change of program rate appears to be excessively high.

The *prior art experience* of the great majority of the John Dewey High School pupils attending the district's eight-year elementary schools has been reasonably typical of the national picture. The district's elementary art supervisor provides a workshop twice a year for the elementary classroom teachers; provides ideas, resources, and special materials for these teachers; organizes traveling exhibits; procures art and art education films; and, when appropriate, procures local newspaper notices. Although the art supervisor has no regular schedule of classroom visitations, the district's elementary teachers make heavy (and welcome) demands on his time by requesting his visits on a consultant basis.

As a result of his efforts and the generally high level of educational background of the teachers, the district's elementary art program contains a minimum of hectographed sheets to be colored in, leather wallets to be stitched and tooled according to commercial patterns, and drawing lessons by formula in the lower elementary grades. There is, instead, considerable emphasis on individual and imaginative two- and three-dimensional expression, some sincere but not often successful effort toward promoting the children's recognition and understanding of the visual arts in their surroundings, and some reasonably effective teaching of the principles of visual organization in the departmentalized seventh and eighth grades. Therefore, the Dewey High students have, for the most part, a fairly wholesome background in art through their prior school experiences. They have made art themselves; seen it in books, in films, and in their community; and may even have gained some insight into how works of art are put together.

On the other hand, their extracurricular art experience is somewhat limited. Except for the children of professional or managerial families, most of the community's youngsters have had no access to art of any type in their homes. Even the do-it-yourself numbered painting and mosaic craze did not seem to affect Las Blusas to any substantial extent. The owner and manager of the local crafts and art supply store can testify to the fact that without his "sideline" of stationery supplies he would soon be out of business. The local theaters studiously avoid "art" films, and a poll of television programs viewed by the local citizens discloses an almost unrelieved pattern of westerns, quiz shows, and crime stories. Consequently, since the schools are not the child's only source of education, it is safe to conclude that the art background of the Dewey High students, while fair, is definitely not rich. Las Blusas is also average, unfortunately, in this sense as well.

Figure 19   Display and storage facilities and work tables in an art room. (Courtesy of New York City Public Schools.)

Extraschool activities are few in number and not too well attended by the student body. Aside from athletic groups and the school orchestra, only the Science Club and the Chess Club draw student support. There has been no art club, nor has there ever been an art service organization.

The *art enrollment* for the previous semester was 327. Classes are held to a maximum of 25 pupils. Grade counselors seem generally sympathetic to the art program and there is no evidence of "dumping" academically slow or discipline problem students into art or crafts, a practice not uncommon in some schools.

Both the *general characteristics of the high school age group and the patterns of development in art* for that age are important data in any analysis of pupils and environment. There are a number of excellent sources available for the former area of information, and a few hypotheses in the second. The builder of a curriculum must select, according to his own educational predilections, the descriptions and ideas in these two aspects. The following descriptive material is not specifically related to our hypothetical community or school. It is presented at this point because pupils in any particular school can be more readily understood if one knows the general characteristics of the school age group.

Without a doubt one of the most important factors in the analysis of the teaching environment is the psychological factor, the patterns of likely behavior based on the age-level and mental, emotional, and social maturity of the pupils. It cannot be stressed enough that these patterns —drawn from data compiled from thousands of adolescents—do not *necessarily* apply to each and every pupil in the secondary school. They are broad guidelines to motivations and behavior rather than "fine-tuned" gauges.

Nevertheless, to know the general characteristics, in psychological terms, is to have some means of insight into the world of the adolescent to which both curriculum and methodology must be related. To know, for example, that most adolescents tend to be hypersensitive about acceptance by the group in which they operate is to insure the insertion of properly structured group activities in the art program. In the same way this item of generally reliable knowledge about the secondary age group can alert the teacher to avoid situations in a class discussion, for instance, in which the individual pupil is forced to act or speak against the interests of the class.

Not *all* adolescents will exhibit these characteristics, but enough of them will so that these psychological generalizations are vital information for the secondary teacher. However, it must be noted that our understanding of the psychology of any group or individual cannot be complete without information about the social environment in which the individual or group has lived or is living. The late C. Wright Mills put it this way:

> It may well be that the most radical discovery within recent psychology and social science is the discovery of how so many of the most intimate features of the person are socially patterned and even implanted. Within the broad limits of the glandular and nervous apparatus, the emotions of fear and hatred and love and rage, in

all their varieties, must be understood in close and continual reference to the social biography and social context in which they are experienced and expressed.[3]

Thus it is only through some knowledge of the general environment of the community of Las Blusas and its people that we can surmise how much of and with what force these general characteristics of adolescents apply to the boys and girls of John Dewey High.

The reader is undoubtedly familiar with at least one of the many fine texts in the area of adolescent psychology. It is, therefore, likely to be unnecessary to do more than briefly review this complex field. There are many schemes for classifying the various age levels and behavior tendencies of adolescence. Divisions into early (13 to 14 years), middle (14 to 16 years), and later (16 to 18 years) appear to be most common in age distribution. Categories such as physical, intellectual, emotional, and social seem to be popular as aspects of the age levels. For our purposes it may be sufficient to summarize by item the wide span of both age level and personality aspect, in an effort to see the development through these years as a totality. The one factor which will be discussed separately is the art development of the adolescent, since it is so obviously significant to the design of curriculum and the selection of method.

1. The adolescent from seventh grade to twelfth is in a phase of physical, and particularly sexual, development of unprecedented intensity. A boy will enter this period a child and leave it a man, both in physical endowment and, in many cases, in emotional maturity. Consequently, these youngsters, particularly in the early and middle period, are inordinately conscious of their bodies and of every aspect of boy-girl relationships. Adjectives such as awkward, noisy, restless, insecure, rebellious, giggly, argumentative, and self-conscious are more appropriate towards the start of this period and become less so as the adolescent years progress.

2. Adolescence, in our culture, is characteristically a period of rebellion against adult authority. For this reason, problems of class control are often aggravated, again more so in the junior high school years and less so as the youngsters move upwards through high school.

[3] C. Wright Mills, *The Sociological Imagination* (New York: The Oxford University Press, 1959), pp. 161, 162.

Figure 20   *Rebound,* a linoleum block print by an eighth grade pupil. (Courtesy of Honolulu Academy of Arts, Honolulu, Hawaii.)

3. The adolescent is likely to have and to show a strong need to be liked and accepted by his peer group. At the same time, his developing sense of individual identity demands overt expression, resulting in frequent conflict most often resolved in favor of the first pressure.

4. The insecurity and conflicts in the individual's relationship to his environment, heightened as they are to this age group, provoke a shifting, almost experimental, attitude towards his own role in social situations. It is almost as if in these years the individual discovers or at least confirms who he is to be and what part he is to play in the adult world around him. This is often apparent in the realms of emotion, sexuality, vocation, politics, and religion.

5. Of overwhelming importance in promoting behavior is the common adolescent need for reassurance of personal worth. To this end the adolescent requires not only attention but recognition. Often, the recognition which cannot be gained through socially approved behavior is won by disruptive antisocial acts. In a sense, it is the fact of the recognition rather than its nature that is of consequence to the youngster.

6. The over-all physical and intellectual growth and development is, of course, a most obvious factor. Because of it, the adolescent in the later period has almost adult capacities in manipulative skills, range of mental potential, and social sensitivity. Sixteen-year-olds have been, not uncommonly, good soldiers, effective fathers and mothers, and creative artists and scientists.

Of greatest relevance to our investigation is the development in art of this age group. A comprehensive analysis of theories about child development in art has been made by Mc Fee.[4] A representative and widely used description is that of Lowenfeld (see Table I).

Whatever the format used to organize the knowledge of the motivations, abilities, and behavior in art of the adolescent, certain minimum empirical observations can safely be described:

1. Along with his burgeoning intellectual and manipulative ability, the adolescent greatly increases his aesthetic sensitivity in this period. Properly guided, he has a growing capacity to respond to works of art of all types and on a high level.

[4] June K. McFee, *Preparation for Art* (San Francisco: Wadsworth Publishing Co., 1961), pp. 147-160.

TABLE 1

SUMMARY   CRISIS OF ADOLESCENCE—THIRTEEN TO SEVENTEEN YEARS

Stage	Characteristics	Human Figure	Space	Color	Design	Stimulation Topics	Techniques
The Stage of Decision Crisis of Adolescence	Critical awareness toward environment and representational outcome. Clearer identification of visual and haptic types or "in-betweens." *Visual Type* Intermediaries: eyes. *Haptic Type* Intermediary: body. Main creative concern: subjective experiences, emotional expressions in which creator feels involved.	*Visual Type* Emphasis on exterior proportion, surface appearance, visual interpretation of light and shadow. Depiction of a moment's impression. Sketchy techniques or realistic interpretations of objective validity. *Haptic Type* Emphasis on inside feelings as contrasted to outside appearance. Depiction of character and expression, often of symbolic qualities. Proportions of value. Individual interpretations.	*Visual Type* Perspective space representation. Apparent diminution of distant objects. Changing intensity with distance. Meaning of horizon. Emphasis on three-dimensional qualities. *Haptic Type* Retrogression to base-line expressions. Perspective of value in relationship to the self. Value relationship of objects to one another.	*Visual Type* Changing qualities of color with regard to environment. Color reflections. Analytic attitude toward color with regard to distance, mood, and so forth. *Haptic Type* Expressive meaning of color. Subjective color expressions. Emphasis on local color. Psychological and emotional significance of color.	*Visual Type* Aesthetic interpretations of form, balance, and rhythm. Decorative quality of design. *Haptic Type* Emotional interpretation of abstract quality of design. Functional design. Industrial design.	Visual and haptical stimulations. Environment and figure. Posing model with interpretations. Sculpture. Graphics. Design. Poster work.	Sketching in crayon. Oil paint. Tempera. Water color. Sculpture in: clay, wood, plaster castings. Graphics: linoleum cutting, etching, lithography, lettering, poster work. Silk screen. Airbrush. Stencil. Design: decorative functional in: stone, metal, glass, textiles, wood, paper, leather.

SOURCE: Viktor Lowenfeld, *Creative and Mental Growth*, rev. ed. (New York: The Macmillan Company, 1957), p. 389.

2. On the other hand, his own productive behavior is most often restricted—particularly at the starting years of puberty—by a rigorously critical attitude. What seventh grade art teacher has not heard a comment similar to "I can't even draw a straight line!" from her pupils? Most frequently, this critical attitude is directed towards representational skill in the areas of drawing or painting. Among more visually sophisticated students it may operate in the realm of design or visual organization.

THE SCHOOL PERSONNEL

The school faculty is the fourth major category to be studied. The total *number* of teachers, including part-time assistants, is 71. The *average age* of the faculty is 32. The *salary range* is from $4,800 to $8,000 in 15 yearly steps. There are three full-time art teachers.

The *educational preparation* of the faculty includes two with doctoral degrees and twenty-seven with master's degrees. All the rest have bachelor's degrees. As in many California schools, teachers have been trained in a wide variety of states and types of schools. Altogether, some 40 per cent of the faculty received their credential training in states other than California.

Within the art faculty itself, only one of the teachers is a product of a California college. Both of the other art teachers attended institutions of higher learning in other parts of the United States—one in Kansas and one in Pennsylvania. All three have master's degrees—the California-trained teacher holding an MFA degree in design, the others having MS degrees in education. They have completed, respectively, 86, 64, and 67 units in fine arts in addition to a similar number of certification-governed units in education and art education. The content emphasis in each case is design, drawing and painting, and ceramics.

All three art teachers are active in the county art association and have exhibited locally. Though they maintain a wholesome interest in personal art activity, each of them possesses the self-image of a teacher rather than that of an artist in the classroom.

The *educational orientation* of the faculty seems to be fairly coherent and wholesome. There are some recognized basic philosophical differences representing primarily the mathematics, science, and foreign language teachers against the remainder of the faculty, the former feeling that their content preparation is intrinsically superior. However,

Figure 21　Another view of a contemporary high school art room. (Courtesy of New York City Public Schools.)

this attitude appears to be more a superficial pose than a serious rift. The majority of the teachers look upon their role as those of guides in the development of children and are quite satisfied with their lot, without either smugness or arrogance.

Personal relationships seem excellent, as manifested by the good-humored and·relaxed atmosphere in the teachers' lounge, where one can find the principal, the custodian, and several teachers enjoying a cup of coffee and a cigarette together. The faculty seem sincerely to like and respect the principal and other administrative and supervisory personnel, who, in turn, all appear to be friendly, always available for requests of assistance, and cognizant of the necessity to support the teachers in any contingency. Discreet questioning reveals the existence of some teachers' "cliques" along the subject matter lines described above and along political party lines as well. In this context, the school role of the art teachers is excellent, there being no patronizing of them by most of the faculty because of their subject.

THE SCHOOL CURRICULUM

The final area of investigation is the curriculum itself. There are three types of high school programs from which students may choose. These are the General, Commercial, and Academic (college preparatory) curricula. About one-third of the boys and one-fourth of the girls plan to go on to college after high school.

The student handbook lists the requirements for each of these programs, in addition to the common core of:

> 3 years of English
> 4 years of Physical Education
> 1 year of Freshman Citizenship
> 1 semester of World Geography
> 1 semester of American Problems
> 1 year of U.S. History
> 1 semester of Driver Education
> 1 semester of Civics (U.S. Government)
> 1 year of Science
> 1 year of Mathematics

There is, quite typically, no required art course in the high school program. A rough count of art students by curricula indicates that equal numbers of pupils from each program take art classes. Boys and girls from each curriculum may "major" in art by taking four one-year courses in art. However, because of the heavy load of specific requirements in both the academic and commercial programs, art majors can, in effect, be recruited only from the general program. Art classes meet one 50-minute period daily.

The *art program itself* is composed of 10 courses, including:

> Art I, "The Fundamentals of Art," (3 sections)
> Art Appreciation
> Ceramics (4 sections)
> Drawing and Painting
> Fashion Drawing
> Advertising Art
> Jewelry (crafts I)
> Leather Crafts (crafts II)
> Weaving (crafts III)
> Graphics

School:
Address:
Phone Number:
Principal: Date:

I. COMMUNITY
    Name, location
    Size of population and area
    Socioeconomic level
    Prevalent cultural patterns
    Educational attitudes and activities
    Community art activities
    School use of community resources

II. SCHOOL PLANT
    Size of plant and grounds
    Condition of buildings and **land**scaping
    Arrangement of rooms
    Art rooms: number and equipment (light, air, display
        space, storage, plumbing)
    Total budget, art budget
    Materials, supplies, and equipment

III. THE STUDENTS
    Number, age, average daily attendance
    I.Q. range and median
    Classroom response
    Prior art experiences
    Extraschool activities
    Art enrollment: total and per-class
    General characteristics for age level
    Art development characteristics for age level

IV. SCHOOL PERSONNEL
    Number, age, salary
    Educational preparation
    Educational orientation
    Personnel relationships

V. CURRICULUM
    General, vocational, academic
    Required pattern
    Electives
    Art program: course offerings and course content
    Supervision

Checklist for environment analysis.

Each course has a content outline filed in the district office. The art department, the senior member serving as nominal chairman, has always considered Art I as a prerequisite for all of the other two-dimensional courses. However, ceramics, crafts, and art appreciation can be taken as individual electives.

There is a district art supervisor for the elementary schools, and the county office has an art consultant who is available on call to the high school art teachers. Occasional meetings of the elementary art supervisor and the high school art teachers are held, and there has been a fruitful exchange of ideas. However, owing to the usual pressure of work, these conferences have been infrequent and, therefore, often repetitious in the necessary review of mutual problems and opinions.

IV

Values: The Keystone of the Curriculum

Values, or objectives, goals, aims, outcomes, have been called the keystone of the curriculum. Without a clear understanding of the kinds of behavioral changes we wish to promote in the learner, it is impossible to construct a coherent and effective course of study. Indeed, it has been the author's observation that art teachers, particularly on the secondary level, can be criticized most severely for a lack of consistent appraisal of *why* their pupils are being motivated, pushed, or guided into specific art experiences.

Before making any analysis of this subject, however, it is necessary to confine our terminology to the most precise available meanings. Therefore, it might be well to point out that a greater-than-usual accuracy may be obtained if we divert the term "values" from its customary synonymity with objectives, and re-define it to mean the "criteria by which objectives are chosen."[1] In this way we will be able to determine those generally applicable principles of behavior which influence our selection of particular facets of growth.

[1] Robin Williams, *American Society* (New York: Alfred A. Knopf, Inc., 1951), p. 374.

Figure 22   Printmaking with string and other textured materials in the high
school. (Courtesy of Kansas City, Missouri, Public Schools.)

The objectives of education are derived from culture. Since the culture consists of the ideals, ideas, methods of thinking, skills, attitudes, institutions, and other man-made aspects of environment, whatever ends the school attempts to achieve will be ends recognized as desirable in the cultural system to which the school belongs.[2]

Broadly conceived, therefore, American education operates within a cluster of values reflecting the patterns of culture inherent in American society. These values have produced, over the span of development of American public education as an institution, a number of criteria for the selection of immediate and long-range goals. Some of these values, as they relate to school objectives, are:

1. Individual personality: an assumed high value placed on the individual as an object of intrinsic worth.
2. Democracy: the maintenance of the maximum of individual self-direction through specific procedures in distributing social power.
3. Science and secular rationality: the specific ordering of experience to provide prediction and control of the environment.
4. External conformity: emphasis on standardized social behavior.[3]

Armed with these values as hypotheses, it is possible to turn to any one of the many compilations of "general purposes" of public education or, more specifically, as we have defined them, "criteria" for the selection of objectives, and observe how it reflects the social values described.

Washton's analysis provides us with a series of such criteria derived from a number of authoritative documents and refined by further questioning. He lists the following sixteen criteria:

To provide students with the necessary knowledge, skills, and attitudes in order that they may:

A. Understand the world of nature, physical and biological, and be able to interpret natural phenomena.
B. Have some appreciation of the background of the civilization which is our heritage.
C. Understand the social, economic, and spiritual forces at work in society and develop a sense of social responsibility.
D. Gain a better understanding of the meaning and purpose of life and a truer sense of values.
E. Participate more effectively in solving problems of contemporary society.

[2] B. O. Smith, W. O. Stanley, and J. H. Shores, *Fundamentals of Curriculum Development* (Yonkers, N. Y.: World Book Company, 1957), p. 107.
[3] Williams, *op. cit.*, pp. 388-442.

   F. Maintain and improve their health and share in the responsibility for protecting the health of the community.

   G. Attain an emotionally stable personality and make a worthy social adjustment.

   H. Utilize a scientific approach in solving problems dealing with society and human welfare.

   I. Be better fit for family and marital relationships.

   J. Communicate effectively through oral and written expression.

   K. Develop a code of behavior which is based on ethical principles consistent with democratic ideals.

   L. Recognize the interdependence of the different peoples of the world.

   M. Recognize and accept one's personal responsibility for fostering international understanding and peace.

   N. Appreciate the best in literature, art, and music, including drama, the dance, radio, and motion pictures.

   O. Discover their own abilities, aptitudes, and interests, and choose a vocation.

   P. To understand the place of the consumer in society and learn to become an intelligent consumer of goods, services, and time.[4]

Without doing violence to the integrity of each issue, these sixteen specific criteria can be summarized by inclusive statements of desirable development:

1. Democratic attitudes
2. Critical thinking
3. Individual knowledge, skill, and appreciation
4. Personal adjustment

If we now turn back to the social values selected as relating to school activity and compare these inclusive statements with them, the similarities are unmistakable.

A wide range of possible objectives can be amassed for the curriculum area of art. As Chapter I suggested, a large variety of old and new ideas exist for the selection of goals in art education.

While prior knowledge of and, indeed, familiarity with objectives used in the past and being used in the present are of tremendous importance to the curriculum planner, it is imperative to realize that objectives must be chosen *within the context of the specific situation*. Just as no one can design the "perfect" or "ideal" curriculum which will operate successfully in any situation, so one set of goals in preferen-

---

[4] Nathan S. Washton, "A Syllabus in Biology for General Education." Unpublished Doctoral dissertation, New York University, 1950, pp. 22, 23.

Figure 23   Tenth grade tempera painting. (Courtesy of Pasadena, California, City Schools.)

tial sequence cannot be listed for all children in all our schools at all times. Rather, the selection of goals of varying degrees of importance is a flexible action dependent upon specific existing variables, such as the grade level, the socioeconomic background of the pupils, the patterns of interest of the pupils, and many other factors.

Taking our cue then from Chapter II and its description of the historical development of ideas in art education, let us examine the range of objectives available for selection in designing a curriculum. If we know the pupils in their environment, we can make intelligent and effective choices in objectives which, once chosen, provide clear guideposts for the enumeration and structure of classroom activities.

Also, in its operation teaching requires some sound distinction between *general* and *specific* goals. As widely understood, general goals are those which are common to most pupils in most learning situations, whereas specific goals have to do with a particular group of pupils in one particular activity. For example, the learning of some of the visual art background of our Western culture may well be a common general objective in all secondary art classes—though of differing importance in various schools. On the other hand, learning to use watercolor paints effectively is a specific objective of one lesson or unit in one class.

Since goals in the art program have to do with the promotion of desirable changes in the behavior (both overt and covert) of individual pupils, it would perhaps be most appropriate to phrase them in individual terms. Although there is little justification for establishing a hierarchy of objectives outside a specific context, certain of these directions of effort might well take frequent precedence in our culture. The following goals will be described in a generally preferential order.

(The Intrinsic Value)

1. *To develop the recognition of the worth of aesthetic experience, particularly through visual means.*

If we assume (and there would seem to be adequate reason to do so) that aesthetic visual experience through the looking at or making of art is of intrinsic value, aside from its historical or developmental benefits, then one of our goals, perhaps of primary significance, must deal with promoting awareness on the part of the pupil of the value in his own life of this type of experience.

Even primitive men do not "live by bread alone," and in our technologically advanced societies, there is need to re-emphasize the broad range of available opportunities for living a full life. It is not that men are crippled by a lack of response to the visual arts, but that their lives are poorer and less varied.

(The Cultural Value)

2. *To inculcate knowledge of and appreciation for the cultural aspects of our own and other societies, both contemporary and historical, in and through the visual arts.*

If education can be said to proceed by the participation of the individual in the social consciousness of the race, the knowledge of any aspect of the activity of men through the ages provides various benefits. Knowledge is of merit for its own sake, in that the acquisition of knowledge, like aesthetic experience, becomes a "good" in itself. Also, when knowledge is accumulated within a coherent framework, it assists insight into the nature of present problems. Furthermore, knowledge constituting "funded experience" enables one to bring to new experiences a means of richer response, as, for example, the greater appreciation developed by historical knowledge of a particular work of art.

It should be noted that this objective suggests far more than simple "art appreciation," although that is an important element. Rather, it is also concerned with the understanding of other aspects of societies through their works in the visual arts. It is a platitude to state how much one can deduce of the life of ancient Egypt from knowing the pyramids, the Sphinx, and the carvings, or how well one can visualize the court life of eighteenth century France from the paintings of Fragonard and Boucher.

(The Developmental Values)

3. *To nurture the capacity for effectively solving visual problems.*

There is considerable reason to assume that one mode, or type, of intelligence involves the solution of problems dealing with concrete objects which we can see, feel, or hear. Since our criteria for the selection of goals includes the development of critical thinking, it should then be self-evident that growth in visual intelligence must become a high priority goal in education. We do not yet know the intimacy of relationship between the various types of problem-solving or, indeed, if there exists any closer connection than that they occur within the same brain. Therefore, we cannot even tentatively assert that the sharpening of one mode of intelligence might influence the strengthening of other modes. However, it is enough to support the development of visual problem-solving on its own singular merit, since visual experiences are incessant companions of all of our waking hours.

4. *To promote the habit of a creative approach to art activities.*

Whatever evidence future investigation may produce with regard to the transfer of creativity from one discipline to another, there can be little doubt that our criteria admit and support the desirability of helping students to achieve some competence in a creative attitude toward the visual arts. Also, while there is still considerable question as to the precise nature of creativity, it is, in its most general terms, a useful concept in explaining the sources of quality and progress in art and in other areas of human effort.

However, it might be of merit to point out that a common misconception of the creative function involves the insistence on originality. In educational terms, creativity should be described as an individual act rather than an original one, since the desired outcome is to attempt to produce what is new to the individual rather than what is new to the culture of the race. Cézannes or Picassos are rare, but every pupil can try to find a solution to a visual problem that is original to him though frequent in historical precedent.

5. *To provide opportunities for the overt expression of emotions in a socially acceptable medium.*

Research during the last thirty years seems to have established beyond question that art activities can supply means for the therapeutic discharge of confined emotions of various types. To manhandle clay, decapitate a parent or sibling in a drawing, or muddy a painting can easily be accepted in a classroom, whereas excessive noise, movement, or violence to one's neighbor must be controlled in any structured group situation. However, the reader must not assume that this concept rests solely upon the seething violence of a so-called Freudian subconscious. Strong emotions of a wholesome and happy nature, which young people are prone to possess, must also be expressed within the same range of alternative media.

Two subsidiary ideas are worthy of mention here. Some measure of therapy can be derived from the use of the pupil's art work as a means of status within the group for children whose academic achievements

Figure 24   Conté crayon portrait by a high school senior. (Courtesy of Honolulu Academy of Arts, Honolulu, Hawaii.)

are less than desirable. Also, the art products of the pupil and his be-havior while creating them can be significant supplementary data for the recognition and diagnosis of emotional problems. A word of caution is essential in this instance. Diagnostic interpretation of art products should be left to those specifically trained for such work. In the over-whelming majority of cases, neither the classroom teacher nor the art teacher is equipped to handle the specialized analysis required.

6. *To assist in the development of manipulative and perceptual skills.*

It should be unnecessary to indicate that deliberate and progressive activities involving skills can promote increased competence in those skills. The particular skills upon which production in the visual arts depend are manipulative and perceptual. The pupil can be trained both to use his hands and to see more efficiently through art activity.

The six goals described all maintain a reasonable consensus of opinion in the literature of art education and among contemporary prac-titioners in the field. Admittedly, there are other goals proposed by some art educators and other writers, both currently and in the recent past. Support of various weight and intensity has been given to such conceptions of aims as the development of patterns of democratic social behavior through art activities, the integration of several aspects of personality, the enrichment and efficiency of learnings in other cur-ricular areas through art work, the revelation of individual truth, the growth of international understanding, the inculcation of moral values, and the presentation of a framework for understanding recent innova-tions in the physical sciences.

While these are all interesting ideas (some more potentially fruitful or more reasonable than others), there is either little rational or empiri-cal validity to their inclusion among goals in art education or any clear assessment of the visual arts in providing them.

It might also be mentioned that the goals listed are not precisely discrete, but interrelated and often interdependent. For example, it is not known to what extent critical thinking in art requires a creative approach to the solution of visual problems. It would seem safe, how-ever, to suggest that there may be a close and significant relationship.

Finally, any formulation of educational aims should be subjected to subsequent critical analysis. The following suggestions can be helpful in such an examination.

If proposed educational objectives are to be considered sound, they must:

1. Be conceived in terms of the demands of the social circumstances;
2. Lead towards the fulfillment of basic human needs;
3. Be consistent with democratic ideals;
4. Be either consistent or noncontradictory in their relationships with one another;
5. Be capable of reduction to behavioristic terms.[5]

The materials in Chapter V, particularly those relating to the selection of course content, attempt to illustrate the impact of the teacher's choice of aims on the art curriculum. Isolating the goals of a teaching-learning situation is by no means an academic pursuit unrelated to the mundane daily *sturm und drang* of school life. Indeed, the aims selected are a vital and integral segment of art education (and all education), in that they impart purpose and meaning into the bustle and activity of the art classroom.

Barkan summarizes the meaning that art can have for education:

> The purpose of a basic education is to achieve some grasp of the full scope of human experience. What often passes as a basic education does, in fact, leave voids in the life experiences of those who are being educated. Human experience is multidimensional; it encompasses concerns that are humanistic in nature along with concerns that are physical, biological, and social. As one of the humanities, the visual arts illuminate significant and unique aspects of human experience; for this very reason they provide an essential dimension of basic education.[6]

[5] B. O. Smith, *et al.*, p. 108 (quoted from Gale E. Jensen, "Methodology and Criteria for the Validation of Educational Aims." Doctoral dissertation, University of Illinois, 1948).

[6] Manuel Barkan, "The Visual Arts in Secondary School Education," *The School Review* (University of Chicago Press, 1962), Vol. 70, No. 4, p. 457.

V

Selection of Courses and Content

The problem of the selection of course experiences, and content within those courses, involves four separate types of decisions:

1. What courses shall be offered in the art program?
2. What particular projects or activities shall be selected within each course?
3. In what sequence shall courses and content be presented?
4. How much time shall be allotted to each project?

It would, perhaps, be most efficient to deal with each question independently and in turn, so that every aspect of decision making in curriculum design is afforded its proper emphasis.

WHAT COURSES SHALL BE OFFERED?

Aside from obvious "studio" categories, such as ceramics, graphics, jewelry, painting, and so forth, there are specific course needs in both junior and senior high schools. For example, on both levels there is need for a terminal course, required or elective in nature. Also, more commonly on the senior high level, a basic course involving training in the principles of the structure of art is necessary for effective achievement in subsequent studio courses. Frequently, for those pupils following an academic or college preparatory high school program, a course in art appreciation or the history of art is of value as groundwork for further experiences in college.[1]

Bearing in mind these special needs, the range of areas in which courses can be offered includes the following:

1. General Art (terminal art course)
2. Art Appreciation (or art history)
3. Art Structure (basic principles)
4. Drawing
5. Painting
6. Advertising Art
7. Industrial Art
8. Theater Art
9. Ceramics
10. Jewelry
11. Metal
12. Leather
13. Wood
14. Weaving
15. Sculpture
16. Photography
17. Graphics
18. Architecture
19. Interior Arts
20. Display Arts (including exhibition)
21. Fashion or Costume Design
22. Textile Design
23. Bookbinding
24. Mechanical Drawing
25. Integrated Arts

Needless to say, more than one course in each area may be needed, and more than one medium may be covered in each course.

We are now ready to use the analyses of Chapters II, III, and IV in order to make effective selections of courses and course content for our hypothetical institution, John Dewey High School, from the list of available courses.

From our investigation of the environment, we know that certain factors will or may relate to the selection of courses in this situation. These are:

1. John Dewey High School has no art requirement. Hence, registration in all proposed courses will be optional.
2. Since the high school is a four-year institution, the age range of the students will be 14-19 years.
3. Since there is no particular art form indigenous to the geographi-

[1] For a report of some experimental curriculum developments in related art courses, primarily for gifted pupils, see *The Bulletin,* National Association of Secondary School Principals, Vol. 45, No. 263 (March, 1961), pp. 18, 19.

TABLE II

SAMPLE ART PROGRAMS, JUNIOR AND SENIOR HIGH SCHOOLS*

Large City

Junior High School

Students: 2115   Teachers: 94

Art Classes	Number of Classes
Art I (required—general art)	9
Art II (elective—general art)	6
Art III (elective—general art)	1
Ceramics	2
Art Craft	1
Art Service	1
Total	20

Senior High School

Students: 2874   Teachers: 112

Senior High Art (elective—general art)	7
Design	1
Ceramics	5
Photography I	3
Photography II and III	1
Painting and Drawing	2
Art Production (art service)	1
Stage	2
Jewelry	2
Life Drawing	2
Year Book	1
Costume Design	1
Design Craft	1
Total	29

* Courtesy Art Section, Curriculum Branch, Los Angeles City Schools.

cal locale, there are probably no courses to which pupils will be attracted because of general environmental influences. The opposite might be the case in other areas of the Southwest; for example, where the weaving, jewelry, and pottery of the Indian peoples constitute indigenous art forms for which the children in that area may have some predetermined interest.

4. The community being lower middle class in socioeconomic grouping, with a significant percentage (approximately 30 per cent) of high school pupils directed toward additional educa-

TABLE III

Sample Art Program, Junior and Senior High School*
(City of 111,000 population)

Art Classes	Number of Classes
Junior High School Students: 666 Teachers: 30	
Arts and Crafts	8
Art	1
Total	9
Senior High School Students: 711 Teachers: 31	
General Art I	3
General Art II	1
Advanced Art	1
Total	5

* Courtesy of Winston-Salem, North Carolina Public Schools.

tion on the college level, there would seem to be reasonable justification and need for an art appreciation or art history course which might be of help in later college studies. Also, the socio-economic level would tend to support a terminal art course for so-called cultural reasons, as opposed to the preeminently "practical" course work preferred by working-class communities. This is not to say that children of lower socio-economic families cannot or should not be exposed to the maximum possible "cultural" influences. This approach would be clearly incompatible with our democratic educational heritage. What should be understood is that the humanities as electives may often be more popular among lower-income-group children when packaged in a more "practical" container.

5. The educational preparation of the art teachers being fairly broad, there are few limitations as to the subjects which they are capable of teaching. One area in which none of the art teachers has had formal training is in photography, which might also be taught in the industrial arts department. It might prove to be of eventual benefit if one of the staff were to take a summer course in photography in order to be able, at some future date, to offer such a class in the high school.

TABLE IV

SAMPLE ART PROGRAM, RURAL SENIOR HIGH SCHOOL*

Students: 327   Teachers: 23

Art Classes	Number of Classes
† Art	1
† Crafts	1
† Advertising Art	1
‡ Undesignated Art	1
Total	4

* Courtesy of Curriculum Section, Kansas State Department of Public Instruction.

† Multiple subject classes of beginning art.

‡ Multiple subject advanced art.

6. The fact that there is a ceramics factory in the town of Las Blusas provides a built-in motivation for student interest in ceramics. While the high school does have a reasonably active ceramics program, it would seem that greater efforts to capitalize on this interest might promote a more extensive program and one of more immediate benefit to the pupils. In this connection, some direct relationship between the management and workers of the ceramics factory and at least one member of the art staff, in the form of class visits to the plant or guest lecturers, might prove fruitful.

These, then, are some of the possible factors influencing selection of courses and content which can be derived from reference to the data collected on the pupils and their environment. As elements of the environment change, it is probable that commensurate curriculum changes will have to be made. Also, an initial survey of the environment, no matter how thorough, may not reveal some relevant elements, which may come to our attention at a later date. It is, of course, desirable to be alert to information obtained through greater insight into a situation and to consciously translate such information, as it is pertinent, into proper attention to and impact on the curriculum.

Recent curriculum planning appears to have, at least in some school districts, re-routed some of the traditional emphasis from a preoccupation with studio activities to verbal and appreciational study in art and in humanities. Hastie and Templeton in their survey of secondary art programs from 1957-1963 discovered new courses, such as *World of*

Figure 25   *Cityscape,* tempera painting, senior high school. (Courtesy of Pasadena, California, City Schools.)

Art in Los Angeles, *Related Arts* in Minneapolis, *Art-Humanities Symposium* in West Hempstead, New York, and *Fine Arts Seminar* in Houston.[2] Frequently, these classes are designed to serve academically talented pupils and just as often they appear to be attempts to stimulate appreciational rather than productive interest on the part of the general student body.

WHAT CONTENT SHALL BE CHOSEN WITHIN EACH COURSE?

Just as environmental factors seem to relate most vigorously to the selection of courses, goals in art education appear to have their greatest bearing on the selection of course content. This does not mean that there is any absolute separation between the two. On the contrary, there is some cross influence in both areas. However, since content selection and goals are closer in relationship, it will perhaps be more useful to consider the availability of content at this point, and then describe the proper weight of values on content selection.

Art education, by virtue of the nature of the subject, is properly concerned with concrete objects. After all, works of art are, either in the viewing of them or the making of them, composed of physical materials (whatever their ideational content). In this sense art is a significantly different discipline than social studies or English or mathematics. One cannot easily talk about art without some visual reference, either on-the-spot or retained in the memory of the audience.

Consequently art teachers, in common with science, music, and physical education teachers, deal with large amounts of equipment and supplies. Also, and more important to our task, the content of art courses tends to deal, initially at least, with materials, projects, and activities. The theoretical range of available content is, of course, infinite. A glance at the list of twenty-five areas from which courses might be selected ought to convince one that listing the particular projects available for each course would produce a virtually endless catalogue of possible activities. For this reason, it would be most practical to select one course, preferably the one with the broadest potential content, and describe the range of materials or processes available for it. Obviously, the general (usually terminal) art course in junior or senior high school is ideally suited to this purpose.

[2] Reid Hastie and David Templeton, "Art Education in the Secondary Schools," *Research Report 1-63* (Minneapolis, Minnesota: University of Minnesota, 1963), p. 17.

Basic materials and processes available for a general secondary art course might include those items listed in Table V.

TABLE V
SOME BASIC MATERIALS AND PROCESSES

Material	Process	Product
Crayon	Direct Batik Scratchboard Melted chips Mixed media	Drawing
Pastel	Direct In wet starch Screen printing Mixed media Conte crayon	Drawing
Ink	Dry brush With pen With stick Wet into wet Scratchboard Felt-tip pen Mixed media	Drawing Painting
Watercolor paint	Direct Dry brush Wet into wet Wash Rubber cement resist Cray-pas Mixed media	Painting
Poster paint	Direct With starch by finger Dry brush Mixed media	Painting
Charcoal	Direct Blending Mixed media	Drawing
Casein	Direct Mixed media	Painting
Oil	Direct Mixed media	Painting
Gouache	Direct Mixed media	Painting

TABLE V (*continued*)

Material	Process	Product
Colored tissue paper	Paint with starch Three-dimensional forms over reed or wire Lacquer to clear plastic Laminated between wax paper Set between layers of Wilhold	Picture Sculpture
Newspaper	Beads Papier-mâché Use as drawing surface Masks (i.e., on plasticene base)	Sculpture Picture
Papers Fabrics Scrap materials	Collage	Picture
Clay	Hand building Throwing Molds Sculpture Mosaics	Picture Sculpture Pottery
Linoleum Wood Inner tube Scrape on cardboard Glue on glass Rubbing Monoprint	Relief Intaglio Lithography Serigraphy	Print
Ceramic tile Glass tile Paper Fabric Edibles Scrap materials Cardboard Wood chips	Mosaic	Picture Sculpture
Paint (oil, watercolor, tempera) Crayon Pastel Paper Mosaic materials	Mural	Drawing Painting Picture

TABLE V (*continued*)

Material	Process	Product
Loom Yarn Leather, metal, etc.	Weaving	Fabric
Wood Papier-mâché Cloth Paper	Puppetry Construction	Puppets Marionettes
Stone Wood (carving, construction, chip mosaic, relief) Soap Plaster (direct, cast, drip, on wire base, mixed with aggregate and cement into sand cast) Wire (mobile, stabile) Clay Plastics Paper Plasticene Salt and flour Sawdust Toothpicks, applicators	Round Bas-relief	Sculpture
Leather	Skiving Stitching Snap setting Lacing Edging Tooling Embossing	Wallet Purse Belt, etc.
Yarn Wood Burlap Cloth Thread	Stitchery	Fabric Picture
Silver Wire Copper enamel Wood Glass Stone setting	Cutting Casting Carving Soldering	Jewelry
Direct On film	Caricature drawing	Cartoon
Film Photographic equipment	Photography	Still picture Moving picture

TABLE V (*continued*)

Material	Process	Product
Cloth Paper Leather	Bookbinding	Book
Pencil Ink Paint Colored paper	Advertising design	Poster Lettering Layout Packaging
Pencil Ink Paint Cardboard Clay Wood Plastics	Industrial design	Drawings Plans Models
Pencil Pastel Ink Paint Cloth	Fashion design	Drawings Patterns Fabrics
Pencil Ink Paint Cardboard Wood Fabrics	Theater design	Plans Renderings Models
Pencil Ink Paint Cardboard Wood Fabrics	Interior design	Plans Renderings Models
Fabric Ink Paint	Printing Painting	Textile
Pencil Ink Paint Cardboard Wood	Architecture	Plans Renderings Models
Metal	Cutting Shaping Etching Forging	Utensils Sculpture
Wood	Carving Construction Burning	Utensils Sculpture

Historically, there are a variety of approaches toward the classification of these materials and processes in a consistent series of groups. Few art teachers will arrange curriculum on the basis of an arbitrary selection of projects. By definition, the design of a curriculum involves some type of pattern of activities. Usually, the pattern will represent some fundamental concept of related groups of experiences. This is,

Figure 26   Architectural rendering by a junior high school pupil. (Courtesy of Wilson Campus School, Mankato, Minnesota.)

of course, almost as much a matter of sequence of content as it is purely selection. However, for the sake of simplicity it would be well to isolate the present discussion to one of content selection, even at the expense of later repetition.

There are at least seven broad approaches to content organization which can be examined individually and in turn.

The Developmental Sequence. Some art courses such as ceramics, graphics, theater arts, and so forth, contain inherent project groupings, in that certain skills or knowledges are necessary as bases for further skills and knowledges. Therefore, the method of organization of content and, of course, the sequence of projects falls "naturally" into place. Whatever other considerations might bear on the organization of content must, with these subjects, assume secondary importance.

Two- and Three-Dimensional Classification. Projects may also be grouped simply by reference to their dimensional attributes. This may be done either by alternating two- and three-dimensional projects for greater interest or by presenting like visual problems needing solution first in one and then another of the two dimensions. While this is a plausible method of content organization, it remains at least superficial in its analysis, lacking an over-all direction.

Design Principles. A more coherent and, fortunately, more common grouping of content is made on the basis of the principles of design. Although there is certainly no general agreement on the specifics of nomenclature, most art teachers would more than likely accept at least a rough division of design factors which would include several elements such as line, form, dark and light, color, and texture. They would also accept several principles such as unity, contrast, and function. No matter how these various elements and principles are named and categorized, secondary course content can be structured along the lines of either each of the elements in turn or each of the principles in turn, with activities calculated to promote recognition and skilled manipulation of the design factors. The assumption on which this type of content organization rests in the terminal art class is that the individual cannot develop any degree of depth of understanding of an art form without some measure of active (what is loosely called "creative") competence in the art form. There is no evidence indicating the validity of this assumption. In fact, general observation would suggest that many of us can develop considerable insight into an art form such as music or literature or dance, without any experience as a practitioner in the form.

However, general observation is not always reliable, nor are all secondary art classes terminal in nature. For students who will take further art courses and, perhaps for those who will not, content organization according to elements or principles of design is at least defensible.

Types of Processes. Another format for the organization of course content is the grouping of projects according to types of art processes. These processes might be drawing and painting, sculpture, graphics, crafts, and so forth, or whatever the art teacher's conception of basic processes suggests. This type of organization also has the advantage of consistency, although it is dependent upon some clear vision of the objectives to be reached in order to be a meaningful pattern.

Social Purposes of Art. The visual arts satisfy certain social purposes in our culture such as advertising, architecture, dramatic presentations, aesthetic experiences of a "pure" nature (in the form of museum exhibits, for example), and others. Course content can be organized on the basis of these or similar categories, giving the pupil added insight into the social role of art.

Areas of Adolescent Art Experience. Almost as a corollary to the previous method, a somewhat similar grouping can be made on the basis of the areas in which the adolescent comes into contact with the visual arts in his daily experience. Starting with the student's home and television and films, and broadening out in ever-widening circles to include art in the total community, content can be organized in clusters of projects in each or some of these areas. This method has, theoretically, the greatest potential for arousing the interest of the student.

Value-Oriented Grouping. A final and probably least common method of content organization is the grouping of projects in the light of the values of art as conceived by the art teacher with his prior knowledge of the specific environmental context. Since this approach is closest to the intent of this volume, it will now be examined in greater detail. It is appropriate to add at this point, however, that these seven methods of content organization are by no means the total possible approaches nor are they mutually exclusive. A sound approach might well be the combination of two of them to offer the maximum coherence to a term plan.

It remains to be noted that there is presently a trend among art educators in favor of a limited range of course content, based on the hypothesis that the values of art can be more effectively obtained from a deep involvement in few media rather than a shallow activity in a vast number of media. This new approach has been stated both as a conceptualization,[3] and as part of the findings in a continuing research on creativity by Beittel and his associates at Pennsylvania State University.

The machinery of selection from the broad range of materials listed involves the careful assessment of the importance of each of the

[3] Manuel Barkan, "Transition in Art Education," *Art Education,* Vol. 15, No. 7, (October, 1962), pp. 12-18, 27.

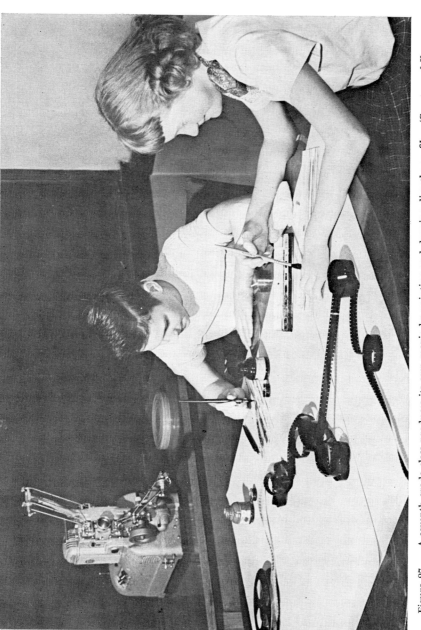

Figure 27   A seventh grade class produces its own movie by painting and drawing directly on film. (Courtesy of Kansas City, Missouri, Public Schools.)

various goals for the specific group of pupils as seen in relation to the particular environment. Let us return to our hypothetical community, Las Blusas, and our imaginary high school. Knowing by now the anticipated group needs of the potential pupils, their general age characteristics, and the demands of the curricular vehicle, the one-shot nature of the general art course, we can suggest that, of the six goals described in Chapter IV, the first one might be of greatest importance. How do we arrive at this conclusion?

1. Since the class is designed as a terminal experience for most of those who will take it, it may represent the last chance for a planned exposure to the pleasure, delight, satisfaction (or whatever term one wishes to propose) inherent in art activity.

2. On the same basis, no other opportunity may appear in the lives of these pupils for some systematic analysis of the rich store of visual arts experiences available to the citizens of the more affluent nations in the world today. This would emphasize the second goal.

3. The pupils coming from a lower middle-class background are less apt to have had prior to their schooling, or to have in the future, any substantial exposure to the visual arts. In the same context, it is necessary to point out that children from higher socioeconomic levels will be more likely to have contact with the arts at home or in the community and that, therefore, these two particular goals would be less significant in that type of environment.

4. While the therapeutic value of art activity can operate in every situation, it is perhaps less vital in relatively average, undisturbed groups. This does not mean that there will be no disturbed pupils in John Dewey High School classes. It is merely suggested that the need for an emphasis on this type of activity may not be as striking.

5. Skill development, while also appropriate to most situations, is, like therapy, a lesser concern for boys and girls who will probably not continue to participate in art activity to any appreciable extent. However, since the secondary school pupil is old enough to be critical of his own production, the teaching of art skills becomes important to ensure the delight and satisfaction to be found in art and is to be stressed as a highly desirable goal.

6. While recognizing the terminal nature of the class in question, and the very real problem in today's secondary schools of finding time for art in the student's already crowded program, the curriculum planner tries to present the most vivid and stimulating content in the hope of creating greater interest in other art classes. By this token, too, the first goal becomes the most vital.
7. Unless substantial evidence can be found that both creativity and the ability to think critically in visual terms carry over from art to other disciplines, these two concepts as goals carry less weight than the first two.

To summarize then, in our hypothetical high school, the intrinsic value, the cultural value, and the developmental value of skill development would seem to be of the greatest importance in the light of what we know about the population of the school. These insights must then be translated into specific types of projects or media which appear to provide the most appropriate means of attaining the goals selected for emphasis. Each medium or project, while it does not induce one benefit exclusively, has greater potentialities for some benefits than for others. For example, most commonly watercolor or tempera painting activities will be more therapeutic in their impact on youngsters than cutting and printing a linoleum block, which provides more skill development and visual problem-solving practice. Usually, such propensities are obvious. Difficulties arise when these proper differences of emphasis in benefit are changed by the backgrounds of pupils. One boy doing the same project in the same class as another boy will obtain an entirely different gain because of the differing extent of what Dewey called his "funded experience," his accumulation of information, attitudes, and previous similar experiences.

A word of caution might be in order. The appraisal of goals in specific contexts is not a matter of elimination but of assigning appropriate weight. All of the six goals described in Chapter IV are desirable in any class. Depending on the particular factors in each situation, some goals become more important than others.

Once we know what aims are of greatest significance to the class and have selected the materials and processes most likely to provide the effective attainment of those aims, we must check the selection against environmental factors such as:

1. Predictable capability of students to use the material.
2. Ability of the teacher to instruct in the use of the material.

3. Availability of the material in the particular school and the appropriateness of room conditions.

4. The investment of time demanded by the material in relation to the total time of the course.

IN WHAT SEQUENCE SHALL COURSES AND CONTENT BE PRESENTED?

The question of sequence has been of some concern in art education. Munro raises the issue in a recent volume, with reference to course sequence:

> The outstanding weakness in present art education, from the standpoint of one who views the whole educational ladder, is its *lack of continuity* from grade to grade. It lacks vertical interrelation, from one rung of the ladder to the next higher one. Education in the arts, as in other subjects, should ideally be cumulative, proceeding step by step without major gaps. The lower steps should function as prerequisites and foundations for the higher ones. Thus interest and momentum in development could be maintained. At present there is very little continuity of this sort in the arts within our school system. . . . A little progress could be made in agreeing on what each course should cover, hence on an approximate sequence of steps. The college teacher who faces a freshman class in either the history or practice of the arts can hardly ever assume any specific knowledge or skill in that field on the part of high school graduates.[4]

The question in the high school is, of course, pertinent primarily to major art programs or to pupils who take more than one or two art courses.

There are at least two alternate approaches to the problem of course sequence:

1. The vertical approach involves the assumption of a developmental pattern in art learning, that is, that some aspects of art must be learned prior to and in preparation for other aspects. This attitude would support the belief that "design" or art structure, in the most sophisticated sense of the terms, is basic to and should therefore precede other particular studio courses.

2. The horizontal approach maintains that the learning of organization in each studio area is separate; that there is, indeed, no developmental pattern. Thus, "design" would be a factor in

[4] Thomas Munro and Herbert Read, *The Creative Arts in American Education* (Cambridge, Mass.: Harvard University Press, 1960), p. 9.

Figure 28   Conté crayon drawing by a high school senior. (Courtesy of Honolulu Academy of Arts, Honolulu, Hawaii.)

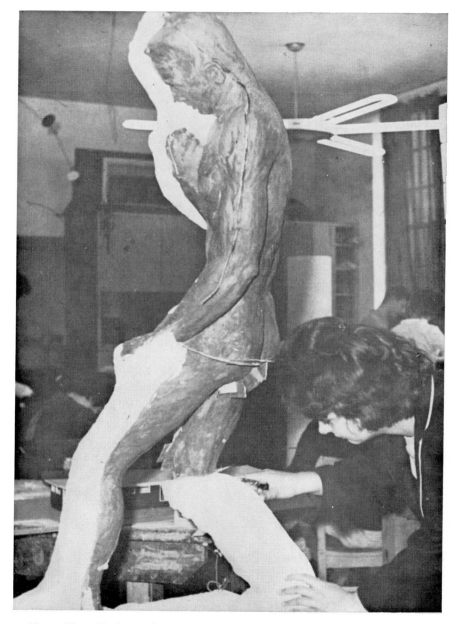

Figure 29   Placing a plaster cast on a clay sculpture in high school. (Courtesy of Berlin, New Hampshire, Public Schools.)

learning each studio field and not common to all or many processes. This concept, strictly held, would lead to a lack of structure in the sequence of art courses.

Since there is no body of research involving this question of sequence, its answer must be left to authoritative or individual opinion, and will depend on the general theories of learning and art of the person making the judgment. The vertical approach would seem to make the most sense and will be recommended here, but with the provision that the judgment is indeed a tentative one.

At best, the total continuity suggested by Munro would seem to be elusive. This is primarily due to the sharpness of distinction between the capacity, interest, and orientation of the elementary child and his older secondary school brother. Probably the most vital of these differences is that the younger child is noncritical or, at least, critical in a very primitive sense. Consequently, the problems he faces in his art activity are, for the most part, nontechnical problems if technical issues are defined as those relating to visual organization and representation.

On the other hand, secondary school youngsters are sharply critical in every technical sense, although they may not be able to identify verbally their own difficulties in art work. The point of differentiation between these two groups, commonly considered to be seventh grade, is undoubtedly an arbitrary location and overlapping in both directions does exist. However, the distinction is valid, and creates apparently insurmountable difficulties in theorizing or constructing any coherent and articulated continuity through the twelve grades in art.

The question of content sequence within courses is often resolved by a decision as to type of content organization. Some of the types of content organization described earlier contain an inherent pattern or sequence of activities. For example, the developmental sequence, the classification by dimensional aspect, design principles organization, and grouping by areas of adolescent art experience, all suggest obvious specific patterns.

The other types of organization in which the effective order of learning experience is not built-in, so to speak, can be sequentially structured on the basis of considerations of motivation. The problem of stimulating and maintaining a high level of interest throughout the semester will probably be the most profitable guide to placement of activities in time order, when that placement is not clearly indicated by the type of organization.

In a seventh grade general art class plan, considerations of motivation might suggest that the first class project should provide rapid and easy achievement and quick surface interest, rather than be a long project demanding greater skill and attention. In the same fashion, a series of projects involving similar materials, such as tempera paint, watercolors, and poster paints, would generally provide less sustained interest than to alternate two- and three-dimensional projects or to insert a gross activity, such as zonolite carving or papier-mâché mask building, between each pair of similar media.

HOW MUCH TIME SHALL BE ALLOTTED TO EACH PROJECT?

The question of allocation of time to the selected course content is perhaps the most difficult to answer definitively. An obvious and important constant in our theories of learning is that individuals learn at varying rates of speed. Any art teacher will testify to the fact that

Figure 30   Making a glass tile mosaic in high school. (Courtesy of Oakland, California, City Schools.)

Figure 31   Seventh grade collage. (Courtesy of University School, Florida State University.)

children complete art projects in widely diverse lengths of time. It would seem impossible to generalize on this issue.

On the other hand, there are several principles which might be of use in approaching this problem.

1. Some processes simply take more time than others for all pupils, because of the size and complexity of the activity or because of the level of precision or care involved. A mural painting is larger than an easel painting. Silk-screen printing is generally a more complex process than linoleum block printing. Copper enamel jewelry usually involves more care than wire jewelry.

2. Projects designed primarily to promote intellectual problem-solving values generally demand and should be allotted more time than those which support, in the main, therapeutic values. The construction of a mosaic panel requires a greater amount of deliberate, conscious planning, and therefore more time, than most painting activities. It might even be said that the benefits which one wishes to have students obtain from an activity requiring careful and thorough planning cannot result from a hurried activity. Conversely, rapidity of action provides just the proper psychological triggering foreseen as the inherent value of a quickly done project.

3. Individual or group interest in or teacher-judged gain from a project might well modify allocations of time, although this element is not easy to predict and include in preplanning. For example, there is merit in having pupils make two or more of whatever they are working on if they show interest in it and seem to be gaining from the experience.

4. Some projects require or can be better done by what is loosely called "research," that is, finding out relevant facts about a project from sources other than the teacher or discovering what others have done with the particular material. These activities also require more time. The painting of a mural, for example, may demand accurate information regarding costume or architectural details, which must be investigated in encyclopedias or other pertinent volumes. Also, carving a block of vermiculite and plaster might be more effective if the student has examined some examples of the kinds of carving previously done with the same material, while the possibilities of a similar piece built with clay are more familiar and obvious.

5. The influence of the teacher, particularly in the type of class-room environment he develops, may promote a range of procedural tempos. Deriving primarily from personality or teaching habits, some teachers seem to approach a classroom of pupils with a sense of urgency, which becomes translated by the class to speedy activity. Other teachers, using the same materials, will appear to be relaxed and unhurried, causing pupils to attack projects with the same deliberate calm. These examples are, of course, extremes. The vast majority of art teachers approach their classes with an attitude toward speed somewhere within the range set by these extremes.

Figure 32 High school students pulling a print. (Courtesy of Berlin, New Hampshire, Public Schools.)

When speaking of time allotment, it is more than just appropriate to mention period length. The average junior and senior high school period is fifty minutes in length. The traditional double period for art appears to be a vanishing phenomenon, due primarily to the sizable problems it raises in total school scheduling. Most art teachers will probably agree that this loss is indeed unfortunate. The fifty-minute period, cut down in work time by distribution and collection of materials and clean-up, introduces an urgency and speed to art classes that is perhaps in keeping with the highly touted rapid pace of contemporary living. However, it is likely that speed is no support to the quality of most experiences, and certainly is not to the production or appreciation of art.

In this connection, it is interesting to note that experimentation in time allotment in the form of flexible scheduling has already revealed possibilities for avoiding the serious pitfall in arbitrary art period length. If in some fashion the pupil's school day can be organized, at least to some extent, on the basis of his involvement in a particular subject problem, such as an art project, rather than on mechanically fixed segments of time, the quality of his experience is likely to be heightened.

Whatever changes in emphasis and direction may be ahead in the curricula of art education, the procedure involved in the design of these curricula will have to be precise, as closely reasoned as appropriate methods of obtaining data allow, and humanistic.

> A true curriculum can only be made by one who knows intuitively what his plan of education will be like in action, what kind of response it can evoke in the learner. The educator must therefore have an image of the child in the reality of his school and his society, at a particular stage in a child's life, and in relation to all the parts of that life.[5]

Secondary art education can make its contribution most effectively when those responsible for its curriculum draw an accurate picture of the learner in his environment and hold it up against the ideal learner in the ideal environment toward which they feel all our efforts must be directed.

The semester plans and course outlines that follow represent course content in several art areas as developed by secondary art teachers in various parts of the country. These plans are not offered here as what should be done in each of these areas, but, rather, as examples of how some classroom teachers view the structure of these classes. The same principle applies to the lesson plans presented in Chapter VI.

[5] Harold Taylor, "The Whole Child: A Fresh Look," *Saturday Review* (December 16, 1961), p. 58.

SEMESTER PLAN

Name of Class: _____   Number of Class Hours per Week: _____

WEEK	PROJECT	MATERIALS
1		
2		
3		
4		
5		
6		
7		
8		
9		
10		
11		
12		
13		
14		
15		
16		
17		
18		
19		
20		

Semester plan form.

SEMESTER PLAN

Name of Class: __Elementary Photography__ (High School)   Number of Class Hours per Week: ___5*___

WEEK	PROJECT	MATERIALS
1	Contact printing — Using their own negatives that have kicked around the house for years. Lecture: First two weeks, organization and attitudes are developed.	Contact paper, contact printer, developing setup.
2	Enlarging — Selective cropping. Lecture: Cropping to add emphasis to art principles. Assign: Shooting a roll of film.	Enlarging paper (medium to high contrast), enlarger and developing setup.
3	Manipulation — Projection Control (P.C.) Lecture: Demonstrate P.C. New approaches to snapshot photos.	Same as above, plus materials used in P.C.
4	Special purpose — Projection Control (Vignetting or an area of P.C. the student wishes to pursue.) Lecture: Developers and Photo papers.	
5	Develop and print roll film. Each student submits four contact prints, selecting one best picture. Lecture: Major evaluation and midterm.	Method used that is easily done at home.
6	Four pictures of people at work. Lecture: List of potential picture material within a limited geographical area that is seen daily. Re-stress art principles.	Projects 6, 7, 8, roll film assigned. Time allowed for selected groups to take pictures on campus during lab. period.
7	Selective seeing — Developed through discussion and examples. Lecture: Lenses, sensitometry, and light meters.	
8	Same subject — Four views and/or angles (people see things differently). Lecture: Studio photography, techniques and lighting. Professional cameras.	
9	Studio shot or free picture. Lecture: Directions in photography today.	Studio, studio lights, studio view camera.
10 – 20	Semester review. Major evaluation. Free time to work in lab. Final.	

*Normal week made up of two class hours of lecture and three class hours of lab. In most cases, two weeks given per project.

Text on approved list for this course is This Is Photography — Its Means and Ends, by Thomas H. Miller & Wyatt Brummitt. Published by the Case-Hoyt Corporation for Garden City Books, Garden City, New York, 1945, 1952, 1955, and 1959.

Courtesy of George H. Dahl, Grant High School, Los Angeles, California.

	SEMESTER PLAN (First Semester)	

Name of Class: <u>Printmaking for Advanced Art Students</u> (High School)   Number of Class Hours per Week: <u>5</u>

WEEK	PROJECT	MATERIALS
1	Lecture and discussions on the many printmaking processes, their unique possibilities for creative expression, the powerful media of communication as used in commercial art, historic development, contribution to social development.	
2	Collect, observe, discuss the different kinds of prints found in books, magazines, posters, pamphlets. Assign individual reports (topic, student's own choice) to be given orally at a later date for class discussion. Make use of available films, film strips, slides, lectures by or visits to local graphic artists. Study contributions of graphic artists of other ages: Daumier, Goya, Hogarth.	
3		
4	Exploration of printing techniques. Stress experimentation and discovery. Study each process as it has been developed and then allow students to PLAY with it. Encourage students to take note of possibilities and limitations of of each media. TEACH PROCESS....NOT TECHNIQUE! They must find their own way of doing things.	
5	Begin with experimental, manipulative activities such as monoprints, build-ups, stamping, pressing, rubbing, rolling.	cloth starch tempera metal cement printer's ink rubber cardboard mineral spirits string rolling pin glass
6		variety of absorbent paper
	Relief prints —	
7	Stress that relief prints can be made from anything that can be carved or molded and can be printed on any thing	wood knives linoleum wood gouges rubber linoleum cutters
8	that will absorb paint. DO NOT STRESS "RULES". This medium is the most effective in showing control and expres-	cork tempera — dry and wet lead printer's ink plaster paper, cloth
9	sion. Each student should make at least 50 prints of one block to show the many effects that can be achieved with color,	clay brushes, rollers White on black
10	value, and texture change. STRESS THE NEVER-ENDING POSSIBILITIES!	Black on white close values of same color, many colors on black painted paper
11	Stencil method — Serigraphy Stress the simplicity of this method. Do not let students become immediately in-	wood wax silk brushes
12	volved and overcome with highly developed precision tools in order to let them explore the medium. Make home-made	squeegee shellac tempera stencil knives paper film paper & adherer
13	frames.	lacquer tusche thinner
14	Lithography — etching — drypoint Stress the unlimited range of value tones these processes offer. Line control,	Metal Litho crayons wax needles asphaltum stone
15	drawing can be practiced and developed.	steel-pointed tools pumice muslin or tar cloth felt acetate nitric acid
16		copper resin zinc soapstone
17	Photograms — photography (Printing with light-sensitive paper) Discuss the photographic process. Try	Dark room and equipment
18	photograms and blueprinting. Use hardware, nature forms, and other objects.	
19		
20		

Courtesy of Marie L. Paul, Englewood High School, Jacksonville, Florida.

SEMESTER PLAN
(Second Semester)

Name of Class: <u>Printmaking for Advanced Art Students</u>   Number of Class Hours per Week: <u>5</u>

WEEK	PROJECT	MATERIALS
1	This semester should be devoted to a more concentrated study of the printing processes. Each student should submit plans for a research project in at least one media in an effort to explore all its possibilities as well as carrying through a creative project of some significance, such as a series of etchings, woodcut portraits, repeated patterns with relief printing, photograms for use in yearbook or other publication, silk screen posters.	
2	Students should help organize and put up instructional exhibit of their work for the whole school to see.	
3	Students should present their research project to the class.	
4	Students should write an evaluation of their own work in printmaking.	

BIBLIOGRAPHY

Books:

Bieglesen, Jacob, <u>Careers</u> <u>in</u> <u>Commercial</u> <u>Art</u>. New York: E. P. Dutton & Co., Inc., 1952.

Herdeg, Walter, <u>Graphics</u> <u>Annual,</u> New York: Hastings House, Publishers, Inc. (yearly).

Lewis, Adele, <u>The</u> <u>Print:</u> <u>An</u> <u>Original</u> <u>Art</u> <u>Form</u>. Studio of Fashion and Art.

Marianaccio, Anthony, <u>Exploring</u> <u>the</u> <u>Graphic</u> <u>Arts</u>. New York: D. Van Nostrand Co., Inc., 1959

Publications:

Cahn, Joshua Binton, <u>What</u> <u>is</u> <u>an</u> <u>Original</u> <u>Print?</u> Print Council of America, 527 Madison Avenue, New York 22, N. Y.

Magazines:

<u>Art</u> <u>In</u> <u>America</u>	Number II, 1960	"Paris letter - Printmaker"
<u>Arts</u> <u>And</u> <u>Activities</u>	Sept., 1957	"How to print from Plaster Slabs"
	Oct., 1957	". . . from way down deep inside"
	Sept., 1958	"Photogrammitical Wizardy"
<u>Design</u>	Sept. - Oct., 1959	"Photograms as an Art Form"
	May - June, 1960	"The Historic Woodcut"
		"Graphic Arts Today"
	Sept. - Oct., 1960	"Sponge and Starch Printing"
		"Printmaking with a Spoon"
		"The Helio-print"
<u>School</u> <u>Arts</u>	March, 1956	"Renaissance in Graphic Arts"
		"Plastic Etching"
		"Making White-line Woodcuts"
		"Experimental Relief Prints"
	April, 1960	"Block Printing Introduces Design"

Courtesy of Marie L. Paul, Englewood High School, Jacksonville, Florida.

SEMESTER PLAN
(Second Semester)

Name of Class: ___Crafts and Sculpture___ (High School)   Number of Class Hours per Week: ___5___
                    1 year course — 1 semester crafts,   1 semester sculpture

WEEK	PROJECT	MATERIALS
1	Ceramic sculpture (additive) Experimental (approx. 1 week)	Clays & Grog — tools & equipment for ceramics.
2	Clay sculptures (approx. 3 to 4 weeks)	
3		
4		
5		
6	Experimental subtractive sculpture (approx. 1 week)	Balsa wood, foam glass, firebrick plaster of paris, wax, and other softer carving materials. Sculpture tools and equipment.
7	Stone, wood and metal sculpture (approx 9 to 14 weeks)	Woods: fruit, elm, mahogany, and softer stones: alabaster, limestone. Metal: lead, aluminum brass, copper, and some welded sculptures. Sculpture tools and equipment.
8		
9		
10		
11		
12		
13		
14		
15		
16	Construction sculpture (approx. 1 to 4 weeks)	Wood and metal, plus miscellaneous materials such as plaster, plastic, aluminum.
17		
18	Research: historical, aesthetic, and technical. (approx. 2 to 3 weeks integrated with sculpture units)	Lecture, slides, demonstrations, movies, field trip, books and magazines.
19		
20		

Courtesy of Richard H. Schwanke, Brookfield Central High School, Brookfield, Wisconsin.

SEMESTER PLAN

Name of Class: Interior Decoration   (High School)   Number of Class Hours per Week: 5
(Each Semester is three 6-week periods)

WEEK	PROJECT	MATERIALS
1	**FIRST SEMESTER:** First Six Weeks:	Discuss decorating a home to suit individual need.
2		Learn to mix color, make color chart, and study color schemes. Study floor and floor coverings. Each student draws out a floor plan of a house on kingston board using ¼"
3		or ½" equals 1' — entirely original or based on a plan found in a magazine. Walls, windows, and doors are constructed of mat board or balsa wood on this plan. Colors are selected and painted on walls, and floor covering is glued
4		down.
5	Second Six Weeks:	Furniture is studied and constructed, and arrangement, lighting, windows, and views are taken into consideration in arranging the furniture.
6	Third Six Weeks:	
7		Accessories are added to the rooms, and the exterior is landscaped, and living and play areas are added. The roof is added last so that it can be moved to view the finished house.
8	**SECOND SEMESTER:** (Same three 6-week periods)	We plan a commercial building in the same manner stated in the First Semester plan.
9		
10	MATERIALS USED:	Kingston board #40 22" × 28"
11		Mat board or balsa wood Wilhold Glu-Bird glue Duco cement
12		Rubber cement Poster paint Acetate .005 (for windows)
13		Mat knife Sample wallpaper books, drapery, and rug materials
14	TEACHER'S REFERENCE BOOK:	Better Homes and Gardens Decorating Book
15	MAGAZINES AVAILABLE TO STUDENTS:	House Beautiful
16		House and Garden The American Home Sunset
17		Better Homes and Gardens
18		
19		
20		

Courtesy of Julia McCann, Central High School, Phoenix, Arizona.

OUTLINE FOR ART APPRECIATION COURSE FOR HIGH SCHOOL

(Grades 10, 11, and 12 - 5 periods a week for 36 weeks)

Basic Understandings - Units I to VI

Unit I.　What is Art?

Difference between art and nature; How are "The Arts" different from other "subjects"? - involvement of BOTH intellect and emotions and, for the creating artist, the physical part of our being too; Visual Art; various types of art expression.

Suggested approach - students fill out questionnaire dealing with the above concepts; group discussion of answers; illustrated lecture and discussion to clarify points of misunderstanding.

Unit II.　Why we appreciate some things and not others. (*15)

Tendency to like what we understand and reject what we do not understand: "story-telling pictures" for example.

Suggested approach - after illustrated lecture and discussion to introduce concept, class members plan and conduct "favorite" picture and "least liked" picture exhibit for school's student body; analyze and discuss results to discover art appreciation level of student body.

Unit III.　How do we widen our appreciation? (*15, *23)

Study, observation, memory, imagination, courageous expression and appreciation, good judgment.

Suggested approach - this is a most important unit for it is here that the students have to be stirred to the point where they are not only interested but eager to learn and experience and discover. A discussion type presentation would probably be best to begin with culminating in the outline plan for the remainder of the course. This will take some doing, for it has to be handled in such a way that the students see that these are the things that they need to know to such a point that they think it is their plan.

Unit III.　How we see things. (*18, *31, *7, *11)

Plastic organization and optical illusion.

Suggested approach - illustrated lecture introducing units IIIA and IIIB.

Unit IIIA.　Optical illusion - perspective. (*31)

Aeriel, curvilinear, and rectilinear perspective.

Suggested approach - experiments in perspective.

Unit IIIB.　Plastic organization - design. (*11, *7, *25)

Design is order; line, area or two dimensions, value, color, texture, volume or three dimensions, and space. Order - harmony, balance, rhythm; harmony of direction, shape, size, color, texture; balance-size and density, color, value, shape, texture, direction; rhythm-direction, repetition, value, color. contrast - difference.

Suggested approach - illustrated lecture introducing each of the above followed by experimental problems in line, area and value, color, texture, planes, and volume.

Unit IV.　Composition (*15, *21b, 22, *7, *11, *18)

Dealing with same things as in the three preceding units. Structure, expression, pattern.

Suggested approach - illustrated lectures followed by experimental problems in composition such as setting in still lifes, landscape and figure composition, three-dimensional compositions.

Courtesy of Bettyne B. Hull, Council Rock High School, Newtown, Pennsylvania.

Unit V. A distinctive way of doing something - Style (*21c, *15, *22)

Overview of "style" in various major art areas.

Suggested approach - illustrated lecture.

Unit VI. What makes a masterpiece? (*21e)

Masterpieces of the past and present including some that were so considered and no longer are for obvious reasons such as Bastien-Lepage's "Joan of Arc in the Garden." Include sculpture and architecture as well as painting.

Suggested approach - illustrated lecture. Group discussion of examples of "masterpieces" which the students question.

Unit VII. Painting

A. What are paintings made of? - materials and (*21d, *24) techniques; gesso, tempera, oils, impasto, etc.

Suggested approach - 1. illustrated lecture
                     2. experiments with materials and techniques.

B. Styles of painting; representative, expressive, analytical, surrealist, etc. (*15, 22, *19, 16)

Suggested approach - 1. illustrated lecture (do not get too technical with each and every "ism")
                     2. experiment with styles of painting
                         (see accompanying lesson plan)
                     3. field trip to museum or art exhibit

Unit VIII. Sculpture

A. What is sculpture made of? - materials and techniques.

Suggested approach - 1. illustrated lecture
                     2. experiments with various materials and techniques.

B. Styles of sculpture

Suggested approach - 1. illustrated lecture
                     2. experiments with various styles
                     3. field trip to sculpture exhibit or "sightseeing" trip to discover
                         various uses of sculpture throughout a city

Unit IX. Architecture (*4, *6)

A. Understanding architecture from a special point of view.

Suggested approach - 1. illustrated lecture
                     2. field trip to experience different feelings which different treatments of
                         internal space arouse and to study use of different kinds of materials
                         and the feelings they arouse
                     3. experiment with architectural design for specific purposes.

Unit X. Printmaking - Graphic Arts (*21a, *27)

A. What are prints made of? - materials and techniques.

Suggested approach - 1. lecture illustrated, not only with reproductions of prints, but examples
                         of materials, tools, and original prints and perhaps demonstrations of
                         printing processes.

B. Prints of past and present.

Suggested approach - 1. illustrated lecture
                       2. experiments with various types of printmaking
                       3. field trip to exhibit of prints.

Unit XI.   Minor Arts. (*2, *17, *9)

A. What are the minor arts? - mosaic, enameling, metalwork, ceramics, jewelry making, ect. Difference between hobby-craft work and minor arts.

Suggested approach - 1. illustrated lecture
                       2. field trip to museum with attention to examples of minor arts; take one
                           or two period rooms and list all examples of minor arts
                       3. experiment with various types of minor arts

Unit XII.   Theater Arts. (*32, *29, *30)

A. "Theater" - past and present and around the world
B. Stage design
C. Costume
D. Props and pageantry

Suggested approach - 1. illustrated lecture
                       2. field trip to a "museum of the theater"
                           (if there is such a thing and if there isn't, it's an idea!)
                       3. field trip to a play or musical which is outstanding from
                           an art point of view
                       4. experiments in stage design, costume, special effects,
                           masks, props and pageantry

Unit XIII.   Primitive Art (*26, *1)

A. What is primitive art? - art of primitive peoples, recent and modern primitives, influences of primitive art on modern art.

Suggested approach - 1. illustrated lecture
                       2. collection of examples of primitive art and examples of
                           influence of primitive art on modern art
                       3. experiments with various kinds of "primitive" art.

Unit XIV.   Our American Art Heritage. (*2, *3, *5)

Overview of America's arts, skills, and artists from past to present with emphasis on 18th and 19th centuries.

Suggested approach - 1. illustrated lecture
                       2. field trip to museum or other area with rich offering of America's arts.
                       3. collection of examples of various types of America's arts and skills
                       4. experience in creating some of the kinds of arts and crafts which are
                         typically American-branding iron designs, samplers, painted tinware,
                         models of wedding chests, slipware pottery, primitive portraits, etc.

SAMPLE LESSON
UNIT VI.   "GETTING TO KNOW SOME MASTER ARTISTS"   SUBJECT: "STYLE" of work

WHAT MAKES "STYLE"?
1. Line or form - which is predominant?
2. Kind of line and/or form -- geometric or curved?   abstract or representative?
3. Composition (arrangement of lines and forms)
     Are they overlapping, scattered, do they have equivocal contours?
4. Pattern - flat or three-dimensional?
5. Tone - strong contrasts or little constrasts?
6. Color - bright or dull, light or dark, warm or cool?

A. STUDY THE WORK OF THE FOLLOWING ARTISTS (use outline above to help you analyze their style)

    (1) Pablo PICASSO
    (2) Juan GRIS (pronounced, Wan Grees)
    (3) Georges BRAQUE (pronounced Jorge Brack)
    (4) Henri MATISSE (pronounced Anree Mateese)
    (5) Paul GAUGUIN (pronounced Gaw gan)
    (6) Paul KLEE (pronounced Clay)

B. Study your own work and see whose "style" your own style seems to resemble most, and write below:

    Your name _____   Artist's name _____

C. Now study the work of your classmates and write beside their number the name of the artist whose "style" you think their style resembles.

1. _____	11. _____	21. _____
2. _____	12. _____	22. _____
3. _____	13. _____	23. _____
4. _____	14. _____	24. _____
5. _____	15. _____	25. _____
6. _____	16. _____	26. _____
7. _____	17. _____	27. _____
8. _____	18. _____	28. _____
9. _____	19. _____	29. _____
10. _____	20. _____	30. _____

D. Write a report including the following:
    (1) Information about the artist whose "style" your style resembles.
    (2) Analysis of what the qualities are in your work which makes it resemble the work of this particular artist.
    (3) Examples of the artist's work
    (4) List of references used for your report.

    Reports should contain about 300 words.

This lesson was preceded by several lessons on space and color organization, painting styles, and still life painting which used musical instruments as its subject. The list of artists would vary according to the student's work. Selections from the work of these artists were chosen by the instructor because the work of this particular group of students most closely resembled the work of these particular artists.

REFERENCES - Art Appreciation Course

  1. *African Sculpture*, Ladislas Segy. New York: Dover Pub., 1958
*2. *Americas Arts and Skills*, Life (ed.) New York: Dutton and Co. 1957
  3. *American Folk Art* from the Abby Aldrich Rockeffer Folk Art Collection, New York: Holt and Co., 1959
*4. *Architecture as Space*, Bruno Zevi. New York: Horizon Press, 1957.
  5. *Architecture of America, The*, Burchard and Bush-Brown, Boston: Little, Brown & Co., 1961.
  6. *Architecture Through the Ages*, Talbot Hamilton. New York: G.P. Putnam's Sons, 1953.
*7. *Art of Three Dimensional Design, The*, Louis Wolchonok. New York: Harper & Bros., 1959.
  8. *Art Today*, Faulkner, Ziegfeld, and Hill. New York: Henry Holt and Co., 1941.
  9. *Chinese Art*, Mario Prodan. New York: Pantheon, 1958.
 10. *Concise History of Modern Painting*, A, Herbert Read. New York: F. A. Praeger, Inc., 1959.
*11. *Design Fundamentals*, C. J. Feldsted. Toronto, Canada: Pitman Publishing Corp., 1958
 12. *Experiencing Architecture*, Steen Eiler Rasmussen. New Y, rk: J. Wiley & Sons, Inc., 1959.
 13. *From Stones to Skyscrapers*, Thea and Richard Bergere. New York: Dodd, Mead, & Co., 1960
 14. *History of American Art*, A, D. M. Mendelowitz. New York: Holt, Rinhart and Wilston, Inc., 1960.
*15. *How to Understand Modern Art*, George A. Flanagan. New York: Crowell Co., 1951.

16. Japanese Painting, H. P. Bowie. New York: Dover Publishing Co.
17. Junior Oxford Encyclopedia, Vol. XII, The Arts. Londong: Oxford University Press, 1954.
*18. Language of Vision, Gyorgy Kepes. Chicago: P. Theobald and Co., 1944.
*19. Masters of Modern Art, A. H. Barr, Jr. (ed.) New York: Simon and Schuster, 1954.
                             (Museum of Modern Art.)
*21. Metropolitan Museum of Art, Art Treasures of the World Series New York: H. N. Abrams, Inc.,
                      1953 and 1954.
    21a. Prints: Techniques and Expression, W. M. Ivins, Jr.
    21b. How to Read a Picture, Wolfgang Stechow.
    21c. Style and Styles, H. W. Janson.
    21d. What Pictures Are Made of, W. M. Heckscher.
    21e. What Makes a Masterpiece", W. M. Ivins, Jr.
22. Metropolitan Seminars in Art, John Canaday. New York: Metropolitan Museum of Art, 1959.
*23. New Art Education, The. Ralph M. Pearson. New York: Harper and Brothers, 1941.
*24. Painting Materials and Techniques - articles on. Utrecht Linens Wholesale Catalogues, 119 W. 57th
                      St., New York 19, N. Y.
25. Pattern and Texture, J. A. Dunkin Wedd. New York: Studio, 1956.
26. Primitive Art, Frank Boas. New York: Dover, 1955.
27. Printmaking Today, Jules Heller, New York: H. Holt and Co., 1958.
29. Scenery Design for the Amateur Stage, Friederich and Fraser, New York: Macmillian, 1960.
30. Scenery for the Theater, Burris, Meyer, and Cole. Boston: Little, Brown, and Co., 1948.
*31. Three Dimensional Drawing, Andrew Loomis. New York: Viking, 1961.
*32. Wonderful World of the Theater, The, J. B. Priestley. Garden City, N. Y. Rathbone, 1959.

Note - Asterisks denote books which are particularly useful.

SEMESTER PLAN

Name of Class: _____ Art 3: Color and Design (High School) _____   Number of Class Hours per Week: ___5___

WEEK	PROJECT	MATERIALS
1	Use primary colors, and mix secondary colors and arrange in a simple color wheel.	Poster paint; soft brush (round); white paper, cardboard for mounting project.
2	Take two complimentary colors and change the intensity by mixing them with one another (12 steps).	Same as above.
3	Make a monochromatic value scale with one color going to black and the same color going to white (12 steps).	Same as #1
4	Create 8 different textures with mixed media (paint, crayon, pencil, pen and ink, etc.).	Poster paint, crayon, pencil, ink, and other media.
5	Make a varied textural composition by mounting varied textural materials (collage).	Sandpaper, cloth, screen, and other textured materials.
6	Arrange many short, straight lines in a peaceful composition, in a festive composition, and a formal composition. Lines should be about 1½" long.	Drawing paper, ruler, and pencil.
7	Using wire, execute an abstract wire construction.	Any type wire that is easy to bend.
8	Do an abstract composition in two colors in which the spaces between forms are as important as the forms themselves.	Drawing paper, paint, brush, (colored paper can be used in place of paint).
9	Create a design showing balance. Use a monochromatic color arrangement with 2 tints and 2 shades.	Poster paint, brush, and white paper.
10	Create a design showing rhythm. Use analogous color arrangement with tints and shades if needed.	Same as above.
11	Create a design showing repetition. Use complimentary color with tints and shades if needed.	Same as above.
12	Create a design showing emphasis. Use complimentary color combined with monochromatic color.	Same as above.
13	Use any one geometric form repeated in different colors on a solid background, creating a spatial composition. Forms must be identical and may not overlap.	Poster paint, brush, or colored paper may be used.
14	Do an accurate pencil drawing of any textured, organic form (bark, marble, rock). Enlarge an interesting square inch of the drawing to 6" square.	Drawing paper, pencil.
15		
16	Create an abstract design and emphasize the color mood, creating a mood with the use of color. Mood that has emotional conotations (sadness, joy, pain).	Poster paint and heavy paper.
17	Create a hand sculpture — the object being to create an object that fits well in the hand and can be transferred into a definite object, such as a door handle, etc.	Plaster of Paris or soft wood.
18	Construct and design an object out of waste materials — either a mobile or a stabile.	
19	Design some kind of play equipment to suit a group of children.	
20	Design, construct, and paint a room arrangement or a window display to scale. Emphasize color, fabric and design.	

Courtesy of Norval D. Carlson, Palo Alto, California, City Schools.

SEMESTER PLAN

Name of Class: ___Seventh Grade Art (general)___   Number of Class Hours per Week: ___3___

WEEK	PROJECT	MATERIALS
1	Contour drawing Form contours (paper)	Drawing paper, pens and ink. Glue, construction paper, assorted string.
2	Lettering practice	Pencil (basic alphabets in notebook).
3	Lettering (a famous quotation)	Pens and ink, drawing paper.
4	Lettering (cut letters)	Scissors, construction paper.
5	Crayon etching Crayon resist	Paper, crayons. Black tempera.
6	Portfolios (for storage of art work)	Cardboard and paper or barrier paper (surplus) and string.
7	Scribble designs (cut and paste)	Construction paper, scissors, and paste.
8	Paper cutting (mural)	Mural paper, tempera paint, brushes, construction paper, scissors, paste.
9	Paper cutting (construction)	Same as above.
10	Toothpick stabile	Round toothpicks, cement (can be painted if desired).
11	Wire sculpture	Assorted wood blocks and wire (various types).
12	Etched metal braclets	Aluminum blanks (can be cut from salvage) asphaltum paint, muriatic acid, steel wool.
13	Animules	Newspaper, wire, string, wheat paste, tempera paint, brushes.
14	Same as above	Same as above.
15	Xmas tree ornaments	Tin snips, tin cans, solder, gold and silver paints, glitter, sequins, various papers, string.
16	Same as above	Same as above.
17	Zonolite sculpture	Zonolite and plaster poured in milk cartons, knives.
18	Drawing and painting	Tempera paints, large brushes. Large drawing pencils, newsprint.
19	Same as above.	Same as above.
20	Same as above.	Same as above.
In general working from projects requiring a great deal of teacher control toward projects requiring more self-control.		

Courtesy of Jo Smelser, East Nashville Junior High School, Nashville, Tennessee.

VI

Methodology

Despite the comparative wealth of literary material devoted to methods of teaching art, at least as compared to the availability of writings about curriculum construction, this aspect of the field is by no means clearly defined. There is, first of all, no coherent position as to what factors in the teaching-learning process can rightly be categorized as "methods." Wynne says about method, "When most broadly conceived, method—often spelled with a capital letter—has reference to the way people are treated."[1] Hughes offers one definition, ". . . discussions of method begin with statements such as 'The details of the procedures a teacher uses to direct subject matter towards the desired end constitute his method.' "[2] He goes on to point out that procedures must be conceived broadly and not limited to teaching aids and discipline.

Here, as in many representative texts on education, methodology is described loosely and not confined to specific elements. It is difficult, however, to examine the scope of theories and practice in a particular phase of a process unless the process itself has been divided into a series of discrete elements. Let us, therefore, review and expand the analysis of Chapter I.

[1] John P. Wynne, *Theories of Education* (New York: Harper and Row, 1963), p. 25.
[2] James M. Hughes, *Education in America* (Evanston, Illinois: Row, Peterson & Company, 1960), p. 425.

A careful analysis of the procedure of the classroom reveals that there are several basic irreducible components. In order for any learning to occur there must be:

1. An aim or aims toward which the effort is directed.
2. Some specific subject matter involving knowledges, skills, or attitudes.
3. A means of arousing and maintaining interest even if it is fear of punishment or failure.
4. A sequence of presentation of the information or content involved and the participation of the pupils in this presentation even if only by looking or listening.
5. Some manner of measurement of the effectiveness of the desired learning. While this last is not absolutely necessary, it would seem pointless in any structured learning situation to anticipate a progression of learnings without some knowledge of achievement at each step.

These five then might be called minimal components of the total teaching process. However, the first component, aims, while capable of having implications for methodology, is logically a preconceived element. It is the "why" of a learning experience rather than the "how." Also, the second factor, subject material, which can also influence method, refers to that which is acted upon rather than the nature of the action. It is the "what," not the "how."[3]

Therefore, it would seem that the last three items of the analysis relate to and constitute the methodology, namely motivation, presentation-activity, and evaluation. Chapter IV and Chapter V tell us about aims and curriculum. This chapter will attempt to describe the available theory on methodology in secondary art, and suggest conceptual foundations on which methods may be developed.

PRESENT VIEWS OF SECONDARY ART METHODS

Recent literature in art education provides some well-supported insight into the methodological process. However, it is interesting to note that some volumes carefully avoid talking about methods of teaching art, as if the conception of the existence of methods is in some

[3] It might be well to remind the reader again that these dichotomies are made for the purpose of analysis and are primarily theoretical. In practice the interrelationship of content and method can be confusingly close.

way reprehensible.[4] It is quite possible that a good many art educators today share this mistrust of methodological dicta. There is no question but that the field has been somewhat over-supplied with "how-to-do-it" materials of book, pamphlet, and periodical article nature. It is also reasonable to assert that much of this material has followed the stereotype of the easy, rigid recipe, providing a crutch for less dedicated teachers rather than a substantial analysis to clarify understandings of the problems involved. Recent educational history has done little to mitigate this attitude towards methodology as a study. It is not inappropriate to point out, for example, the present day opprobrium in which "methods courses" in teacher training institutions are held, both by critics of the public schools and by the public at large.

Nevertheless, there is a legitimate study discernable in methodology and one which is vital to the task of teaching art in the secondary school. Specific problems of motivation, presentation, and evaluation do exist and demand solutions whatever name is given to the problem area.

Perhaps the most inclusive review of methods is to be found in de Francesco's book in which he lists some of the several methods used by teachers as ". . . directed, correlated, integrated, free-expression, and 'core' teaching." He describes the directed method generally as "formal and authoritarian", the free-expression method as dominantly a laissez-faire approach, core teaching primarily as the solving of problems based on common learnings, integrated teaching as the involvement of a multiplicity of subject areas which are tied together in the mind of the learner and correlated as the employment in art of the incentives induced in other subjects.

He goes on to provide psychological bases for relating methods to particular groups of children, specifying *motivation* as the guided development of interest and purpose, *stimulation* as the release of innate needs and goals, *integration* as the unification in the learner of his knowledge and attitudes. Both the art of questioning and group processes used as means to support these methodological processes are examined.

In a separate section, de Francesco reviews the problem of evaluation in art, summarizing it as substantially a process of guidance.[5]

[4] In two recent volumes (Wickiser, and Conant and Randall) the word "method" is not to be found in either the Table of Contents or the Index.

[5] Italo L. de Francesco, *Art Education: Its Means and Ends* (New York: Harper and Brothers, 1958), pp. 133-229.

Figure 33   Textile print by a seventh grade pupil. (Courtesy of Honolulu
Academy of Arts, Honolulu, Hawaii.)

Munro in a recent volume[6] presents three ways of teaching the arts, namely practice, historical, and theoretical. While these categories are not clearly methodological, bearing heavily on the nature and structure of the curriculum, their implications for methods cannot be ignored. In an earlier work Munro specifies as principles of methods "progressive differentiation and specialization" and "increasing purpose and systematic control."[7]

Finally a comprehensive and psychologically structured analysis of the secondary student is included in Lowenfeld's classic work.[8] The most significant aspects of his view include the observation of the development of critical awareness in the adolescent and the absorption of the adolescent in his relationship to society. Again, while these are broadly conceived premises, they are immediately relevant to conceptions of method.

It would appear, therefore, that in terms of the analysis organized in this chapter, posing a pattern of motivation, presentation, and evaluation, the literature in art education is not particularly helpful. While there are many relevant concepts about methodology, there is an almost bewildering lack of precision in its structure. As in the case of curriculum, although even more widely, a great deal has been said about the subject but very little on the subject.

This lack of precision is primarily caused by a consistent confusion of the components of the teaching situation. The two components most often confused—not necessarily incorrectly since as has been stated before they are closely related, but fruitlessly so for analytical purposes—are content and method. Thus, when a writer discusses an integrated arts course as a method of teaching, for example, he is by no means inaccurate. Broadly conceived, integrated material does constitute a "means" of teaching. Nevertheless, a higher degree of precision in analysis can serve to make our understanding clearer. It is no more difficult or cumbersome to think of the integrated arts course material as curriculum, and the ways in which the teacher arouses interest in the material, presents it to the pupils and guides their activity, and evaluates their learnings, as the methodology involved.

[6] Thomas Munro and Herbert Read, *The Creative Arts in American Education* (Cambridge, Mass.: Harvard University Press, 1960), pp. 16, 17.

[7] Thomas Munro, *Art Education, Its Philosophy and Psychology* (New York: The Liberal Arts Press, 1956), pp. 18-22.

[8] Viktor Lowenfeld, *Creative and Mental Growth* (New York: The Macmillan Company, 1947), pp. 256-391.

Figure 34   Wire and wood sculpture, high school. (Courtesy of Berlin, New Hampshire, Public Schools.)

METHODS OF TEACHING ART

What then can safely be said on the subject of methods? It might be well to start with some basic assumptions regarding methodology. While these ideas are neither definitive nor specific, they can serve as guides for a subsequent focus on the particulars of method.

1. Since secondary youngsters are for the most part well into that phase of child development stressing self-critical awareness, motivation, presentation, and evaluation must be couched in reasonably sophisticated and intellectualized terms. Unlike the elementary teacher, the secondary art teacher can no longer anticipate pupil spontaneity as an ally in the struggle to promote interest, attentiveness, and acceptance.

2. Methodology being almost uniquely personal, in that it reflects the way in which individual teachers teach, is theoretically unlimited in its diversity. The identical patterns of motivation, presentation, and evaluation might easily be or appear to be radically different approaches between any two teachers because of the impact of personality. A tone of voice, a choice of words in a question, even a look while examining a youngster's project, can easily alter the most concise and rationalized method, even, at times, inadvertently.

3. Like aims and curriculum, methodology is primarily dependent upon the specifics of physical, psychological, and sociological circumstances. As in the survey of bases for curriculum decisions, the art teacher must take the factors described in Chapters III and IV into consideration when selecting procedural or methodological techniques. Bearing this need in mind, Chapter VI attempts to display a range of possibilities in method, so that the selection process can reflect choices from a richer span of possibilities.

4. The reduction of methodological elements to the three of motivation, presentation, and evaluation, is not meant to ignore or deny other concepts of methodology either implicit or stated, such as the ones quoted from the literature of the field. This is the way one teacher analyzes the problem of HOW to teach art. Just as teaching techniques vary from person to person, conceptualizations about teaching techniques are essentially individual.

MOTIVATION

Perhaps the most startling and vivid statement that can be made about motivation as a factor in the learning process is that ideally it should be nonexistent as a concern for the teacher. That is to say, all pupils should come to school each day imbued with a fervent desire to learn all that is available for them to absorb in the school day. There is, of course, no need to remind the reader that this is certainly not the case in our schools today (nor for that matter, has it ever been the case as far as history tells us).

The reasons for the considerable lack of "built-in" motivation among our pupils are both sociological and psychological in nature and while fascinating are not relevant to this volume. It is enough to say that the art teacher in the American secondary school is faced with the problem, in varying degrees of complexity, of devising means of developing and maintaining the interest and attention of her pupils in the activities planned for each day.

It is at this point, when faced with the most crucial problem of education, the desire of the learner to learn, that we can begin to distinguish a variety of methodological approaches. There are three broad lines of approach, namely formal, informal, and functional. The formal approach to teaching method is, of course, the oldest and probably still most common over the world. It might be called in another context the "traditional" or "directed" method of teaching and can be characterized in its purest form as that attitude which supports an authoritarian classroom structure in which an adult-determined (teacher, supervisor, or other adult source) curriculum is imposed upon the pupil. Formal methodology ignores motivation except insofar as fear of failure or punishment is concerned, phrases its presentation in unabashed dictatorial terms, and makes its evaluation precise and objective. This method substantially does not concern itself with the varying interests of pupils nor with differing abilities or rates of learning.

This word picture might well evoke the visual image of the dunce-hatted pupil seated on the stool facing the corner of the room, and the reader may ask whether this situation in the extreme form described exists any longer in our classrooms. Probably not, at least in the United States, so pervasive have been the influences of educational philosophers, such as Dewey, of new knowledge about the process of human learning, and of the expansion of the child population served by our public schools. Nonetheless, the formal method of teaching veers in the direction of the model described above, as theoretical as that model may presently be.

The informal method of teaching is, again ideally, the direct opposite of the formal. Its historical designations have been "laissez-faire" or "free-expression." Here the classroom situation is an unstructured as possible. The aims and curriculum can be much the same as those which other methods use, but the motivation of the child is self-sought and self-discovered, the presentation is individual (with teacher help), and the evaluation is based on self-judgment. An extreme example of this method can be found in *Summerhill*.[9] Just as the formal method is teacher dominated, the informal method is child dominated.

The third approach, the functional, can be said to be the mid-point between the extremes of rigidity and license. Here aspects of motivation, presentation, and evaluation are related functionally to the other factors of the educational process, the WHO, WHAT, and WHY. If, for example, a reasonably normal class situation prevails, the teacher using this method will attempt by some device to arouse the interest of her pupils in the project they are to start that day. If, on the other hand, the class is overcrowded and liberally weighted with problem youngsters, the teacher may adopt a more authoritarian approach in order to ensure the continuance of orderly and purposeful activity. And, lastly, in the instance of an honors class of dedicated students, the teacher may well employ an informal, almost laissez-faire, method with success.

The reader is reminded that the former illustrations are oversimplified, although their broad outlines are not inaccurate. The problem of selecting a method of teaching to fit a given situation can be quite complex.

These then, in brief, are the three main types of methodology in teaching. Let us focus now on the issue of this section which is, properly, motivation.

Assuming a functional method of teaching, there are a variety of means which can be used to promote the interest of secondary pupils in art activities. These means can be generally divided into two categories, intrinsic and extrinsic motivation. These two terms are perhaps old-fashioned in their flavor and have definitely lost caste in the heir-

[9] A. S. Neill, *Summerhill* (New York: Hart Publishing Company, 1960).

archy of educational jargon. However, they are eminently appropriate to this issue since they clearly distinguish between the kinds of interest aroused by the motivational device, intrinsic having to do with interest in the art activity for its own nature, and extrinsic relating to an interest in the art activity for outcomes external to its own nature. It should be unnecessary to add that for most art teachers developing intrinsic motivation in productive or appreciational art activities is generally preferable to the alternative. Art should develop meaning to young people for itself rather than for outside values.

To be specific then, there are several types of motivational activities in each category. It may be useful to examine each of these devices with some care, since much of the success or failure of an art activity can be dependent upon its motivation.

Intrinsic Motivation

Probably the most effective device for stimulating interest in an art activity is the *demonstration*. Even the most blasé adolescent cannot help but marvel at the seeming miracle of a pot form rising out of the swirling clay on the potter's wheel. This technique permits the art teacher to make good use of what is probably his greatest asset, his art skill, and to focus it on the point at which it will be of the greatest service, the interest of the pupils.

However, it should be noted that the demonstration need not necessarily be done by the teacher himself. It can be carried out by a professional artist or a more experienced student, since it is simply an enactment of a process of art activity in front of a class. Its most important criterion, in order to serve a motivational purpose, is that its staging convey as much as possible of the drama of the creation of a work of art. For those who have seen "The Face of Lincoln," which is essentially a filmed demonstration by sculptor Merrill Gage, the fascination of watching the personality of Father Abraham emerge from a mass of amorphous clay can readily serve as a stimulant to personal effort with the same medium.

A second sort of intrinsic motivation consists of *visual materials:* films, slides, filmstrips, photographs, and works of art themselves, either done by professional artists or by students. Though rarely as effective as the demonstration (unless the film includes shots of the process), visual materials do direct attention to the work of art. It should be unnecessary to state that whatever the nature of the visual material it should be of the highest aesthetic quality obtainable.

A third type of intrinsic motivation involves *verbal activities* and could range from a talk given by a visiting artist to a discussion on an issue in art by members of the class. Here again, while the emphasis may not be on the process of creating the art work, interest is at least concentrated on some aspect of the art work. One device used by some teachers, and for purposes other than exclusively motivational, is to display the portrait of or an art work of a specific artist each week and then start each week (or each day, for that matter) with a short verbal presentation on the life, times, and work of that artist. It should be obvious that this device also serves to develop some learning in art history and can be used to promote a group identity and greater calm at what is usually the restless start of a period. Two points should be noted here. First is that it would be extremely difficult to use a purely verbal motivational process in an art class. Art is, after all, a visual medium, and to only talk about it can be extremely limiting. In fact it might prove interesting to try to teach an art class for one period, past the initial roll call, without using any words.

Second is that motivation can be obtained indirectly. Pupils can become interested in painting a watercolor not only through watching a demonstration of watercolor painting, but through hearing about the life of John Marin or Winslow Homer or discovering the uses of watercolors in advertising.

Extrinsic Motivation

The most extreme form of extrinsic motivation is, of course, the fear of punishment or failure discussed relative to the formal method of teaching. However, less violent means can be marshalled towards the end of arousing interest, one of them being *rewards*. An anecdote may best illustrate this technique:

> During the depression years, a young woman just graduated from a teachers college was appointed to a rather "difficult" all-boys high school in a large city. Her first day was catastrophic, leaving her in near-hysterics. The foreign language classes could, at least, be controlled by grades, but the twenty-minute home room in the morning and fifteen-minute home room in the afternoon were a shambles. Her principal did not expect her to return the next day.
>
> The next morning, to his amazement, not only was she in her classroom, but her home-room rowdies were silently immersed in

Figure 35   Junior high school scratchboard drawing. (Courtesy of Long Beach, California, City Schools.)

encyclopedias and other reference volumes.

How had this overnight miracle occurred? Our resourceful young teacher had purchased a series of tickets to the local baseball games and a large set of puzzle books. She had offered a ticket each week to the boy who did the most pages in the puzzle book. A clear case of professional survival through the use of extrinsic motivation.

The foregoing anecdote does not, of course, set a standard any teacher would like to follow. It was a measure justified by desperation only, and reflecting circumstances that are, fortunately, uncommon. Ideally, learning is its own reward.

The most prevalent type of extrinsic motivation through reward is via grades. Again, while this type of interest is not the most desirable, it is at least a form of interest, and art teachers faced with difficult situations use it. It would seem reasonable to suppose, however, that the quality of the art experience may well be greatly inferior when the creator is concerned with the mark he is to get rather than the satisfaction of creation.

A second type of extrinsic motivation is the stress on the *ultimate use* of the particular project. This type takes at least two forms: 1) the ultimate use of the product, and 2) the ultimate use of the skill or knowledge involved in the project. A high school class can become enthusiastic about a jewelry project when it is pointed out to them that the end product—pin or ring or cuff links—can be given as a gift to a boy friend or girl friend. In the same fashion, interest in an interior-design project can be generated once youngsters are convinced that they can transfer this ability from the classroom to their own rooms at home.

Underlying all of these motivational devices is the one essential ingredient in this phase of methodology—teacher enthusiasm. Without it most of these techniques can easily be unproductive of the desired results. With it they are sometimes unnecessary. The art teacher who can be sincerely excited by the wonder of art and by the thrill of seeing his pupils experience this wonder, can infect a group with the same feeling. At times this is the only motivation that is needed.

The lesson plans at the end of this chapter provide examples of carefully prepared motivations illustrating some of the types described. Good teaching involves knowing what types of motivation are appropriate for specific groups of pupils and what constitutes undermotivation and overmotivation. To hold up a few examples of the previous products of a particular activity and to expect an enthusiastic response

Figure 36   An example of senior high school photography. (Courtesy of Los Angeles, California, Public Schools.)

from a class is at least unrealistic. On the other hand, to present a long series of visual and verbal devices focused on a particular process is to run the risk of tiring the class. The best methodological advice that can be given is the admonition: "Teacher, know thy pupils."

PRESENTATION

That segment of a one-period lesson or a several-period unit, lasting from the close of the motivational activity to the start of the evaluation, if there is one, can be called the "presentation." In most art classes, this is roughly the studio portion of the period during which the productive work is done. Like the teaching-learning process itself, the presentation can be broken down into constituent elements which include at least 1) giving specific directions for the project, 2) distributing (then later collecting) the materials used, and 3) supervising the activity of the class.

As in the case of motivation, the presentation can show the influences of variations in methodology. The formal method demands strict control and limitation of the pupils as they go through the class period. Just as in lieu of motivation the formal method would suggest a command ("This morning we are going to . . ."), elements of the presentation take on the character of a teacher-imposed and teacher-dominated activity. It is easy to think of the formal presentation activity in the light of a caricature so that any description sounds overstated. Yet prior to the era of what can loosely be called modern education, art classes (indeed, all classes) followed a pattern of dictated presentation, limited materials, and regimented activity.

It might be of interest to illustrate the impact of differing methodologies by describing a hypothetical art class taught in each of the three methods. To make the illustrations sharper in comparative significance, it might be well to label each class as to the period of recent history it represents.

> *Class A:* After calling the roll, Miss Dobbs cleared her throat. "This morning," she announced sternly, "you are going to make an ornamental design as a border for the page of lettering you did last week." She interrupted herself to call out sharply, "Henry, put your pencil down and fold your hands on the desk in front of you."
>
> Henry, she mused, was a most ill-behaved boy, uninterested in art and unwilling to be attentive. She wondered if the I.Q. test score could have been an error in his case. If so, she did not want him in her class. After all, art was not for just any pupil in high school, only for those with superior intelligence and ability.
>
> "In order to select design units for the border," she continued, "you will make a practice drawing of four geometric forms. Remember that you will have only one sheet of paper. Don't waste it!" Carefully and deliberately Miss Dobbs placed one sheet of paper on

each desk while the two girls who were her monitors distributed the sharpened pencils, rulers, and the soft erasers. "Place the date, April 25, 1928, on the bottom left-hand corner of your paper," she directed and then sat down at her desk in the front of the room to await the raised hands and the trips to her desk by the less confident pupils.

While she waited, Miss Dobbs considered questions she might ask on the written test she would give the class at the close of the lesson. She tried hard to be fair to the children and the number grades on the project itself should, she felt, be supplemented by a verbal quiz. While she was not an artist herself, she had taken a major of twenty-four units in art in college and felt well qualified to make the judgments necessary for teaching her art classes.

Class B: Miss Bobbs came into her third-period art class late. The boys and girls were gathered around a table watching the antics of a beetle incarcerated in a tall jar. One of the boys glanced up at her. "Greetings Harriet," he called out, "what are we doing today?"

She smiled warmly at the upturned faces. "What would you like to do, boys and girls?" Fred wanted to discuss the recent invasion of Poland by the Nazi armies, but Alice suggested they work on the classbook. Knowing Alice's interest in having her free verse printed in the classbook, the pupils indulgently supported her wishes in a rapid voice vote. Fred and Harvey, undaunted, retired to the rear of the classroom to carry on their discussion uninterrupted by their peers.

Some of the students brought out boxes of charcoal and sets of poster colors and brushes. Miss Bobbs sat down at one of the rear tables to describe to a group of her youngsters the ballet she had seen the night before. Alice worked for a while rather feverishly on several charcoal drawings to illustrate her poetry. When she brought the drawings back to Miss Bobbs, the teacher looked at them, tilting her head pertly, and asked, "Alice, how do you *feel* about these sketches?"

Meanwhile, most of the class worked on a variety of projects a few of which were only loosely related to the classbook. They were unhurried and, in some cases, uninterested, knowing that their teacher expected them to discover and fulfill their needs individually. Some of them were continually unsatisfied, but even these were not critical of the teacher. Miss Bobbs might be ineffectual, but she was so obviously sweet and so very fond of each of them.

Even Billy, whose pegged pants served as a badge of his social attitude, was tolerant of the teacher. He read his comic books (between trips to the boys' room for a smoke) in arrogant disdain of his human environment. Miss Bobbs had promised him he would "find himself" eventually. He had kept his immediate response, "who's lost?", inaudible.

Class C: By the time the late bell rang all the pupils were in their seats staring expectantly at Miss Hobbs, who was carving with great absorption on a rough block of what looked like concrete but gave way to her knife like soap. She smiled and waved to the class while the attendance monitor quietly marked down the absentees in the class roll book. At last Miss Hobbs put down her knife and exclaimed, "Well now, almost finished." She wiped her hands on a paper towel and smiled at the class.

"Does anyone recognize the ancient civilization this sculpture I'm copying comes from?" There were several guesses: Egypt, the Pacific, Africa. "You're the closest Tom," she said. "This is one of my favorite pieces of sculpture, a statue of Quetzalcoatl, the chief god of the Mayans, from Teotihuacán in central Mexico. Notice how simple and almost geometric the modulations of the form. That's why your guesses were all of primitive societies rather than of Renaissance Italy, for example." Miss Hobbs went on to contrast the pre-Columbian carving with examples of sculpture from 18th and 19th century Europe illustrated by large mounted photographs.

In the middle of her description, one of the students asked almost impatiently, "But Miss Hobbs, what's the stuff you're carving made of? It looks like rock and it cuts like butter."

"I'm glad somebody finally asked that question," she answered, and the class laughed. She described the ingredients and mixing procedure of the vermiculite block. "So that we can get started on our carving right away, I had the advanced art group mix some blocks for you. I hope they're set. There's a block for each person. Those who enjoy working with this material can come in after school today and mix a larger block for a more ambitious pieces of sculpture. Who knows, there might be a Michelangelo among us!"

At her direction, three pupils began to distribute the materials for the period: newspaper to cover the tables, dull knives for the carving, and the vermiculite blocks themselves. The class started to work eagerly, and Miss Hobbs went around from table to table trying to spot problems before they occurred and to give whatever added stimulus an extra few words would provide. She knew the weaker students who would lose interest rapidly and kept her eye on them.

"Admiral Rickover should try this for a week," she mused to herself as she moved quickly from table to table.

Again, the first two of these fanciful narratives are about as subtly drawn as cartoon stereotypes, and they present the extreme of each viewpoint. It would, perhaps, be safe to say that today the vast majority of the secondary art teachers' approach to methodology would cluster most thickly around the functional. Directions for the activity are

Figure 37   Pen and ink portrait drawing by a junior high school pupil. (Courtesy of Honolulu Academy of Arts, Honolulu, Hawaii.)

clear-cut and posed, whenever possible, as the response to a problem phrased by the class. When it can be done, an activity is described in a historical context. Visual aids are as plentiful and as high quality as the teacher's resources permit. The distribution of materials and their subsequent collection is as unobtrusive and mechanical as a well-organized class can make it. And once the pupils are engaged in the art activity the teacher's role becomes, if anything, many times more active in that he must 1) continue to motivate on an individual level wherever interest seems to lag, 2) provide guidance with the art procedure, with problems involving the materials being used, and with personality conflicts, and 3) observe and record, either with mental notes or on paper, the progress of the project for subsequent evaluative purposes.

As analyzed here, the presentation-activity portion of a lesson is to some extent a matter of what in educational jargon is called class management. More than in most subject areas, the art teacher faces the problems of physical and human relationships within the classroom. To solve these problems he must be firm without harshness, well prepared without seeming mechanical, and incessantly alert. Contemporary methodology in art education would seem to be more demanding than it has ever been, both in subject and in professional preparation.

EVALUATION

This final segment of methodology in the teaching of secondary art involves two major problems: 1) On what bases is performance or achievement in art to be judged? and 2) How can the judgment be measured? These are complex problems, dependent upon, and more clearly than most problems identified with, the teacher's basic philosophical position. An unbiased student of the recent literature in art education can justifiably note a tendency to restore what some feel to be necessary high aesthetic criteria to the high school art program.

As an example of this tendency, here is one rather intemperate indictment of contemporary art education:

> In summary it would seem that our high school art program is structured on a faulty philosophic base characterized by a denial of the plastic arts as a disciplined form of expression worthy of a place in the curriculum on its own merits, And in its place we have art that is "fun," capable of mastery without effort, of use in preparing consumers of things and capable of being taught by people unprepared to make a meaningful statement in any media and yet expected to teach in many areas.[10]

[10] David Manzella, "The Time for Fundamentals," *Art Education J. of NAEA,* Vol. XIV, No. 2 (February, 1961), p. 27.

Surely this statement attacks the entirety of the art program, its aims and content as well as its methods. However, it is not until we come to the evaluation of student work that the implications of this point of view become clear and decidedly problematic. Few art educators would deny some merit to the directions proposed by the statement. But to follow it all the way brings us to the problem of evaluation. If we make art "a disciplined form of expression" in the high school curriculum, how can we judge and measure the work of the pupils?

To begin with, it might be of help to develop some comprehensive concept of the purpose of evaluation, both in the sense of judgment and measurement. De Francesco sees the process of evaluation as primarily for the purpose of guidance.[11] For the pupil, the teacher, the parent, and for peripheral agencies, such as administrators and supervisors, the results of an evaluation should provide insights for further action. If Johnny receives an "A" in advertising art (whatever the bases of judgment or measurement), the grade as information should be useful to guide one or more of the people involved. Perhaps Johnny will want to take another art class. His teacher might feel his approach to the course and to this pupil was justified. Johnny's parents may encourage him to major in art.

Or, if a judgment is made without the rigidity of measurement by grade, it can still serve the guidance purpose just described through a summary statement by the teacher or by the pupil himself as to the progress being made. The pupil (and his parents) will then know what still needs to be studied or practiced, and the teacher will know how to help the pupil.

If, then, the purpose of evaluation is to guide those involved in the teaching-learning process, what are the bases on which judgments can be made? The classical answer to this issue is to refer back to the aims of the particular activity, to ascertain the degree of correspondence of the outcomes of the activity to its preconceived or developed-in-process goals. Thus in a life drawing lesson, for example, if the specific objectives include the development of skill in drawing the human figure, the evaluation can at least start with some form of judgment and measurement, if desired, of the amount or degree of skill gained through the activity.

Surely this type of judgment seems a simple enough affair. All

[11] De Francesco, *op. cit.*, p. 229.

the teacher needs to do is to examine the product and judge it loosely ("This second drawing shows considerable improvement over the first"), or measure it on an appropriate scale of letter or number grades. Yet, as the chapter on values indicated, the aims of an art program are multiple and diverse. In addition to the pupil's growth in knowledge and skill, art experiences are provided to support intellectual development, extension of creative ability, emotional expression, the recognition of the worth of aesthetic visual experiences, among others. True, some of these may be general in nature rather than specific to the particular problem but they are relevant issues to evaluate. Without them, only partial judgments are being made.[12]

It is here that the significant distinction between judgment and measurement becomes most apparent. In most objectives or areas of growth, judgment, which is primarily individual, is difficult but not impossible. Measurement, on the other hand, is primarily comparative, as between one student and another, and is as accurate as the precision of the scale used.[13] Most art educators will agree unequivocally that there are as yet no significantly valid or reliable objective tests or scales of measurement in art. To compare one youngster's art work with that of another is to render an almost wholly subjective decision with all of the attendant probability of error.

Further, even if a substantial test in design, for example, existed, how can the art teacher compare one pupil to another? Let us say that Henry is a gifted and capable designer whose work is first rate, but who is uncooperative, indolent, and rude. George, conversely, is a model pupil, industrious, disciplined, and courteous, but inept in his ability to organize the elements of the visual arts. Whose grade should be higher?

If we go back now to the statement quoted at the start of this section, we can see that one school of thought might lead to a heavy emphasis on aesthetic criteria. Henry, in this approach, would receive the higher grade. Other art educators will disagree, urging that George's effort and intent is as important as Henry's ability, if not deserving of greater reward.

Again, analysis by types of methodology begins to resolve the many issues of evaluation. The informal method of teaching art tends to

---

[12] De Francesco divides this area into various elements of growth: mental, emotional, social, physical, aesthetic, and creative.

[13] It is true that judgments can also be comparative, while measurement can be individually contained. The terms are used here in their most common meaning.

restrain evaluation to a minimum and to limit it to a self-administered and self-scaled action. Only judgment is involved here. Rarely will the informal method admit comparisons of pupils.

Formal method is frankly competitive. Judgments are usually manifested by measurement, and measurement is seen as rigid, objective, and accurate. A formal teacher would tend to place the accumulation of knowledge and the growth of manipulative skill as the highest values in the hierarchy of educational aims.

In contrast to both these points of view, functional methodology supports evaluation of all pertinent facets of the pupil's growth, shifting its emphasis on what is of greatest importance from one lesson to the next. It recognizes the lack of objective scales in art, except in obvious areas, such as historical data and art terminology, and tends to restrict measurement to the least possible within the total educational context. It encourages self-judgments by youngsters, but does not absolve the teacher from his responsibility to decide the achievement of his pupils.

Functional method in evaluation suggests the following criteria both for judgment and, when necessary in the school situation, for measurement by grade:

1. Interest
2. Effort
3. Expressiveness of work
4. Imaginativeness of (or originality or creativity of) work
5. Ability to solve visual problems
6. Knowledge of art
7. Manipulative skill

According to these criteria the secondary art teacher can judge the growth of each of his pupils. In some projects one criterion becomes of greater importance than the others. The last in a series of watercolor painting projects can emphasize either imaginativeness or expressiveness, assuming some minimal degree of skill with the technique has been developed in the earlier works. The evaluation of a weaving activity can stress the pupil's ability to solve visual problems, whereas a project in leather might stress manipulative skill.

Also, flexibility in the preference of criteria is related to the type of class in which the evaluation takes place. A seventh grade required art class will necessitate a heavier accent on interest and effort than a pre-professional 10th, 11th, and 12th grade class in fashion illustration.

Figure 38   Papier-mâché mobile, junior high school. (Courtesy of Long Beach, California, Public Schools.)

At the present time, functional methodology also assumes that measurement, in the sense of an exact weighing of the criteria listed, is futile if not detrimental. Nonetheless, most school district policies require letter grades in secondary school art as in English or social studies, and the art teacher must temper his viewpoint with discretion. Eventually, as our society matures and permits educational practice to catch up with theory, arbitrary letter grades will give way to individual reports of a more substantial nature. In the interim, the art teacher

Figure 39   Preparing paper sculpture decorations for a Christmas banquet in senior high school. (Courtesy of Kansas City, Missouri, Public Schools.)

will have to transpose his judgment of the pupil to a grade in the manner least offensive to his conscience.

One final point must be made regarding group evaluations of pupil work. This type of evalution made by the total class or by a select number, a jury, can be a useful instrument since it can provide fresh insights for both pupil and teacher. Even the experienced teacher can frequently be startled by the acute perceptions of the adolescent. However, a poorly organized or ineffectively moderated evaluative discussion can be disastrous. It must not be allowed to turn into competitive criticism or reciprocal adulation. At best, the pupils can verbalize, and thereby clarify, their own conceptions of the outcomes of both the process and the product of the art activity.

The following lesson or unit plans, like the semester plans presented in Chapter V, offer examples of how some secondary art teachers structure classroom art activities.

No amount of planning or knowledge of method can supplant the imaginative, interested, and courageous teacher. When all art teachers, and all other teachers for that matter, are unrestrained and daring in their manipulation of the classroom, when they are genuinely absorbed in the maturation of their students, and when they are bold in striking to the heart of vital human issues, this type of volume may be of little purpose. It is to be hoped that this time may come soon.

LESSON PLAN	
Name of Class: _____ Grade: _____	
Project: _____	
Objectives:	
Materials:	
Motivation:	
Presentation:	
Evaluation:	

Lesson plan form.

LESSON PLAN

Name of Class: ___Art___	Grade: ___8th___

Project: ___Mask Making___

Objectives:	(1) To develop a fuller understanding of masks from past civilizations. (2) To lead the student to discover that creating can be fun. (3) To acquaint the student with a variety of new materials. (4) To give him experience with modeling design in the third dimension.
Materials:	Newspapers Cardboard scraps Strings Paper towels Wheat paste Tempera paint Brushes
Motivation:	The Loon's Necklace film followed by discussion of Indian masks and their significance. Showing of African masks under opaque projector and discussion of this type. Display masks made by other students from previous year.
Presentation:	Some students sketch their mask before beginning. Each student makes a large paper wad of dry newspapers the shape of mask, and wraps it with string to hold shape. Begin with torn strips of newspaper dipped in wallpaper paste. Put on one vertical layer, the second horizontal, etc. After about six layers have been applied, cut nose, mouth, etc. out of scrap cardboard and adhere with strips of newspaper dipped in paste. Cover mask with several more layers of strips and paste. Use strips of paper towel for final coat. When dry, cut out back with knife and remove insides. Put strips over cut edge. Paint with tempera; add hair, jewelry, etc.
Evaluation:	We display our masks in the classroom for a few days, and discuss them as a class. Later they are moved to the lunch room for display.

Courtesy of Jo Smelser, East Nashville Junior High School, Nashville, Tennessee.

LESSON PLAN   Page 2

Film:

The Loon's Necklace

Encyclopaedia Britannica Films, Inc.
Wilmette, Ill.

Discussion of Indian Masks and their importance.

Books:

African Sculpture

Ladislas Segy
Dover Publications, Inc., New York

Discussion of African Masks and their importance. (Show some pictures from book under opaque projector.)
31 pages print - 163 pages of illustrations.

Other Reference Books:

Exploring Papier-Mâché

Victoria Bedford Betts
Davis Publications, Inc. (1955), Worcester, Mass. 134 pages.

Mask Making

Matthew Baranski
Davis Publications, Inc. (1955), Worcester, Mass. 101 pages.

LESSON PLAN

Name of Class: ___Art___ Grade: __7th & 8th__

Project: ___Dry-point Etching___

Objectives:	To involve the student in creating his own etching for the purpose of helping him both to appreciate the qualities of a print and to understand the process of printing.
Materials:	Etching press or wringer press. Etching tools or darning needles with balsa handles, one tool per student. Lucite or acetate, .025 gauge, two 18 × 24 inch sheets cut into 4 × 5 inch pieces. Water-soluble block printing inks, two 2-ounce tubes of black. Rags, for rubbing excess ink from etching plate. White drawing paper, 150 sheets. Two packages of paper towels for blotting paper. Sponge, water, scissors, masking tape.
Motivation:	Since a multitude of old and new prints are available, these provide a valuable source of motivation for the child. However, since etching is a relatively new experience to the junior high school student, the process itself is fascinating. The desire to see that first etching is sufficient encouragement.
Presentation:	1. The first step is the etching of the drawing on the plastic plate. 2. The moistening of the paper. 3. The inking of the plate and the rubbing off of the excess ink. 4. The printing of the plate.
Evaluation:	The etching process, while it demands some skill, offers the student a variety of art experiences. The student must draw as well as design. He must be careful with the various tools, techniques, and materials, since carelessness can mean the difference between a successful or an unsuccessful print. The quality of an etching is evaluated by the following methods: 1. The lightness or darkness of the individual line is dependent upon the deepness of the cut. Therefore, a vague image will result from a plate in which the lines are not deeply incised. 2. The amount of pressure produced by the printing press will determine the degree of sharpness in the print. If there is insufficient pressure, the image will become indefinite. 3. The amount of moisture on the paper effects the print. If the student is using a water base ink and has used excess moisture on the paper, the print will be blurred. 4. The leaving of some ink upon the flat surface of the plate will aid in producing mood or tonal effects. However, since this technique requires skillful handling, it should be employed only after the student has learned to properly handle the printing of line.

Courtesy of Jack Lerman, Haven Junior High School, Evanston, Illinois.

LESSON PLAN

Name of Class: ___Art History and Appreciation_____ Grade: __9 – 12__

Project: ___Prehistoric Art___(beginning of a full year course based on studio methods.)_____

Objectives:	To give the students knowledge of the beginnings of art in prehistoric times.
	To give the students an understanding of the metaphysical, religious, and superstitious uses of art in a primitive society.
	To teach prehistoric art through studio techniques, as well as lecture and discussion.
Materials:	Flagstone, nails or hard sticks, bacon grease, old broken pastels and colored chalk (earth colors), stencil brushes, tubes or straws, sticks, etc.
	Bibliography dealing with cave paintings and primitive art.
	(Life Magazine series on Epic of Man.)
Motivation:	Discussion and visual illustration of the rituals and uses of the cave paintings, early hand prints, bear claw scratches, etc. Discussion and demonstration of how color comes from the earth. Discussion of sources in dreams of ghosts, animal gods, and superstitious beliefs of early man and primitive societies. Discussion of astrological signs, zodiac, and metaphysical forces which ruled man.
Presentation:	Choose a flagstone slab or anything similar and flat.
	Grind up old pastels and chalk into dust (or use different colored dirt), place hand on stone, smear surface with bacon grease as a substitute for mammoth oil) and either blow colored powders through the tube or apply color with stencil brush around the hand.
	With a nail or hard stick scratch the symbol of the zodiac sign, or animal they have as a pet, or would create a god of as their favorite animal, or pet they have lost and would find again and keep power over. This is done over the top of the hand print.
	With the stencil brush and the bacon grease, add color to the animal design.
	These can be mounted on boards and hung on the wall, coated and used as paperweights or, if large enough, as door stops or floor sculptures if they stand up alone.
Evaluation:	Self-evaluation and discussion on what has been learned about the metaphysical uses of art, how well they understood the relationship between what they did and what primitive man did.
	Teacher evaluation on how well the student seemed to identify himself with the project (if possible) and used the natural materials for purposes of visual expression.

Courtesy of Robert J. Saunders, Commack Senior High School, Commack, New York.

LESSON PLAN	

Name of Class: ___Advertising Design___ Grade: ___9 – 12___

Project: ___Use of Dry Printing in Advertising___

Objectives:	1. To show how in advertising, printmaking is used starting with one of the first basic forms of printmaking, the dry print. 2. To satisfy the artistic growth of the student with the use of usual materials in an unusual way related to a specific problem in advertising. 3. To show the student how abstract symbols are used in the practical field of advertising. 4. To train pupil in basic principles of good design related to a technique of printing.
Materials:	Large white paper (colonial or antique white) Pencil Either: paraffin (preferred), wax, crayon, or soap Colored chalk
Motivation:	Review four principles of design Show reproductions of graphic design executed by famous artists with which students are familiar. Show specific examples of printmaking used in magazines and brochures, including woodcuts, etchings, etc.
Presentation:	1. Each student is given two pieces of paper. 2. Draw with pencil on each paper an abstract design that is related in feeling and structure. 3. Color-in first design with a thick layer of chalk to enhance particular feeling of design. 4. Rub over chalk design with thick layer of paraffin. 5. Take second pencil design and place face up on waxed chalk design surface. 6. With a pencil, rub over pencil lines and areas of second design — the pressing attaches wax and color to the back of second design and takes from or leaves on negative area on first design. 7. Separate two papers.
Evaluation:	Comparison of two designs showing how one contains line and the other form. Review elements and principles of design. Class critique on each design.

Courtesy of Walter E. Rutkowski, North Attleboro High School, North Attleboro, Massachusetts.

LESSON PLAN

Name of Class: ___Commercial Art 1_____ Grade: ___10 – 12___

Project: ___Sketch Pad Cover Design_____

Objectives:	1. Cover design to show use of pad. 2. Cover design to be reproduced in one color. 3. Cover Design to be commercially acceptable for sales and promotion purposes.
Materials:	1. White poster board. 2. India ink or poster paint. 3. Tracing paper flap (for corrections by the instructor).
Motivation:	1. Pad to be used by students. 2. Examples of past student work. 3. Examples of professional sketch pad covers. 4. Cash award (special job agreement with a local firm to print winning entry). In our case, students received $24.pp total cash awards plus a finished printed sketch pad for each participant.
Presentation:	1. Present examples of cover designs and explain merits of each. 2. Discuss with students the objectives of project. 3. If a local firm is involved, have representative speak to students. 4. Request students to observe display of sketch pads in local stores and make a verbal report.
Evaluation:	1. Since judging was done by a retail firm handling the sketch pad, reasons for selection of winners needed to be known. The paper firm representative evaluated each design for the class. 2. Factors such as the flexibility of the design for different sizes of pads were discussed. 3. Students of commercial art and other art classes evaluated the attractiveness and commercial effectiveness of each design submitted before they were judged.

Courtesy of Yoshio C. Nakamura, Whittier High School, Whittier, California.

LESSON PLAN

Name of Class: ___Interior Decoration_____ Grade: __10 – 12__

Project: ___S & H Green Stamp Unit_____

Objectives:	To take a catalogue and select room furnishings from the limited possibilities listed. To determine the value and questionable savings of savings stamps. To develop a sense of selectivity in choosing furniture, etc. To develop an informed consumer approach to buying and saving.
Materials:	S & H Green Stamp Catalogue. Illustration board, watercolor paper, charcoal paper, pen and ink, watercolors. One month's supply of groceries, cleaning, gas, etc., and the sales receipts. Various periodical articles dealing with savings stamps.
Motivation:	Discussion of the overwhelming presence of savings stamps, gimmick advertising, and give-aways. Discussion of the problems of chosing furniture and decorating a room with a limited line of selections.
Presentation:	Have the students select from the green stamp catalogue (only one catalogue to a student) enough furniture to furnish a room: living room, bedroom, kitchen, recreation room, bathroom, etc. For one month prior to the project, have the students collect receipts for all purchases which have green savings stamps given away with them or list the money spent for such items. From this data determine the amount of stamps accumulated. When the room has been furnished, determine the amount of stamp books necessary to accumulate the furniture, and then from the monthly average spent determine how long it would take to save all the stamps. Visual project: From the selections made, design a room either in a two-dimensional drawing or build a model of the room with models of the furniture built from the pictures in the catalogue. On a side chart show pictures of each item selected from the catalogue cut out in paste-up. A written statement, either separate paper or lettered into visual project.
Evaluation:	Student discussion and evaluation of the project and what they learned about decorating a room, building a model, of consumer awareness, and new attitudes to saving stamps, if any. Teacher evaluation: Review of written statement and month's work, and skill and methods used by the student to illustrate the room designed, as well as the appropriateness of each item selected for the room being furnished.

Courtesy of Robert J. Saunders, Commack Senior High School, Commack, New York.

Bibliographies

bibliography A

General Art Education

ALSCHULER, ROSE H., and HATTWICK, LA BERTA W. *Painting and Personality.* Chicago, Ill.: University of Chicago Press, 1947, Vol. I and II, pp. xi and 590.

Art Education in a Scientific Age. Kutztown, Pa.: State Teachers College, Eastern Arts Association Yearbook, 1952, pp. 112.

Art Education Today. New York: Teachers College, Columbia University, 1937, 1938, 1940, 1941, 1942, 1943, 1948, 1949-50.

BARKAN, MANUEL. *A Foundation for Art Education.* New York: The Ronald Press Co., 1955, pp. xi and 235.

———. *Through Art to Creativity.* Boston, Mass.: Allyn and Bacon, Inc., 1960, pp. xii and 365.

BURKHART, ROBERT C. *Spontaneous and Deliberate Ways of Learning.* Scranton, Pa.: International Textbook Co., 1962, pp. xx and 260.

CANE, FLORENCE. *The Artist in Each of Us.* New York: Pantheon Books, Inc., 1941, pp. 370

COLE, NATALIE R. *The Arts in the Classroom.* New York: The John Day Co., Inc., 1940, pp. 137.

D'AMICO, VICTOR, WILSON, FRANCES, and MASER, MAUREEN. *Art for the Family.* Museum of Modern Art, Distributed by Simon and Schuster, Inc., New York, 1954, pp. 110.

DEWEY, JOHN. *Art and Education.* Marion, Pa.: Barnes Foundation Press, 1947, pp. vii and 315.

———. *Art as Experience.* New York: Minton, Balch & Co., 1934, pp. vii and 355.

DOW, ARTHUR WESLEY. *Theory and Practice of Teaching Art.* New York Teachers College, Columbia University, 1912, pp. 73.

DUNNETT, RUTH. *Art and Child Personality.* London: Methuen & Co., Ltd., 1948, pp. vii and 72.

EDMAN, IRWIN. *Arts and the Man.* New York: The New American Library of World Literature, Inc., 1949, pp. vii and 144.

157

Erdt, Margaret. *Teaching Art in the Elementary School.* New York: Rinehart and Co., Inc., 1954, pp. xiii and 284.

Gaitskell, Charles D. *Children and Their Art.* New York: Harcourt, Brace & Co., Inc., 1958, pp. xiv and 446.

Gray, Wellington B. *Student Teaching in Art.* Scranton, Pa.: International Textbook Co., 1960, pp. xviii and 154.

Haggerty, Melvin. *Art—A Way of Life.* Minneapolis, Minn.: University of Minnesota Press, 1935, pp. 43.

Hartman, Gertrude, and Shumaker, Ann. *Creative Expression.* New York: The John Day Co., Inc., 1932, pp. 350.

Jefferson, Blanche. *Teaching Art to Children.* Boston, Mass.: Allyn and Bacon, Inc., 1959, pp. viii and 294.

Keiler, Manfred. *Art in the Schoolroom.* Lincoln, Neb.: University of Nebraska Press, 1951, pp. 214.

Klar, Walter, Winslow, Leon L., and Kirby, C. Valentine. *Art Education in Principle and Practice.* Springfield, Mass.: Milton Bradley Co., 1933, pp. viii and 422.

Landis, Mildred M. *Meaningful Art Education.* Peoria, Ill.: Charles A. Bennett Co., Inc., 1951, pp. 185.

Lanier, Vincent. "Doctoral Research in Art Education," University of Southern California, 1962, pp. 52.

Lindstrom, Miriam. *Children's Art.* Berkeley, Calif.: University of California Press, 1957, pp. 100.

Lowenfeld, Viktor. *The Nature of Creative Activity.* New York: Harcourt, Brace & Co., Inc., 1949, pp. xvii and 272.

———. *Your Child and His Art.* New York: The Macmillan Co., 1954, pp. 186.

Manzella, David. *Educationists and the Evisceration of the Visual Arts.* Scranton, Pa.: International Textbook Co., 1963, pp. xiii and 97.

Mattil, Edward L. *Meaning in Crafts.* Englewood Cliffs, N. J.: Prentice-Hall, Inc., 1959, pp. ix and 133.

McFee, June K. *Preparation for Art.* Belmont, Calif.: Wadsworth Publishing Co., Inc., 1961, pp. xiv and 341.

McIlvain, Dorothy S. *Art for the Primary Grades.* New York: G. P. Putnam's Sons, 1961, pp. xix and 297.

Mearns, Hughes. *Creative Youth.* New York: Doubleday, Page and Co., 1925, pp. xv and 234.

Munro, Thomas, and Read, Herbert. *The Creative Arts in American Education.* Boston, Mass.: Harvard University Press, 1960, pp. 65.

Neice, Robert C. *Art: An Approach.* Dubuque, Iowa: William C. Brown Co., 1959, pp. 142.

Read, Herbert. *Education Through Art.* London: Faber & Faber, Ltd., 1943, pp. xxiii and 320.

Schaefer-Simmern, Henry. *The Unfolding of Artistic Activity.* Berkeley, Calif.: The University of California Press, 1948, pp. xii and 201.

SCHINNELLER, JAMES A. *Art: Search and Self-Discovery.* Scranton, Pa.: International Textbook Co., 1961, pp. xxix and 322.

SCHULTZ, HAROLD, and SHORES, J. HARLAN. *Art in the Elementary School.* Urbana, Ill.: The University of Illinois Press, 1948, pp. 103.

VIOLA, WILHELM. *Child Art.* Peoria, Ill.: Charles A. Bennett Co., 1944, pp. 206.

WHITFORD, WILLIAM G. *An Introduction to Art Education.* New York: D. Appleton-Century Co., 1929, pp. xvii and 337.

ZIEGFELD, EDWIN, and SMITH, MARY E. *Art for Daily Living, The Story of the Owatonna Art Education Project.* Minneapolis, Minn.: University of Minnesota Press, 1944, pp. 155.

bibliography **B**

Secondary Art and Education

Art in American Life and Education, National Society for Study of Education, Fortieth Yearbook. Bloomington, Ill.: Public School Publishing Co., 1941, pp. 819.

CONANT, HOWARD, and RANDALL, ARNE. *Art in Education.* Peoria, Ill.: Charles A. Bennett Co., Inc., 1960, pp. 345.

CONANT, JAMES B. *The American High School Today.* New York: McGraw-Hill Book Co., Inc., 1959, pp. xiii and 140.

D'AMICO, VICTOR. *Creative Teaching in Art.* Scranton, Pa.: International Textbook Co., 1942, pp. ix and 261.

D'AMICO, VICTOR, (ed.). *Visual Arts in General Education.* Commission on Secondary School Curriculum, Progressive Education Association. New York: D. Appleton-Century Co., 1940, pp. 166.

DEBOER, JOHN, (ed.). *The Subject Fields in General Education.* New York: D. Appleton-Century Co., 1941, pp. ix and 239.

DE FRANCESCO, ITALO L. *Art Education, Its Means and Ends.* New York: Harper and Brothers, 1958, pp. xix and 652.

HUGHES, JAMES M. *Education in America.* Evanston, Ill.: Row, Peterson & Co., 1960, pp. xiii and 496.

INLOW, GAIL M. *Maturity in High School Teaching.* Englewood Cliffs, N. J.: Prentice-Hall, Inc., 1963, pp. xii and 467.

KRUG, EDWARD A. *The Secondary School Curriculum.* New York: Harper and Brothers, 1960, pp. xi and 555.

LOGAN, FREDERICK. *Growth of Art in American Schools.* New York: Harper and Brothers, 1955, pp. xiv and 310.

LOWENFELD, VIKTOR. *Creative and Mental Growth.* New York: The Macmillan Co., 1957, p. xxii and 541.

MUNRO, THOMAS. *Art Education, Its Philosophy and Psychology.* New York: The Liberal Arts Press, 1947, pp. xvi and 387.

RANNELLS, EDWARD W. *Art Education in the Junior High School.* Lexington, Ky.: University of Kentucky Press, 1946, pp. 127.

REED, CARL. *Early Adolescent Art Education*. Peoria, Ill.: Charles A. Bennett Co., Inc., 1957, pp. 236.

SMITH, B O., STANLEY, W. O., and SHORES, J. H. *Fundamentals of Curriculum Development*. Yonkers, N. Y.: World Book Co., 1957, pp. 685.

STRATEMEYER, F. B., FORKNER, H. L., and McKIM, M. G. *Developing a Curriculum for Modern Living*. New York: Teachers College, Columbia University, 1947, pp. xiii and 558.

This Is Art Education, National Art Education Association Yearbooks 1951-1961, Kutztown, Pa.: State Teachers College.

THOMAS, L. G., KINNEY, L. B., COLADARCI, A. P., and FIELSTRA, H. E. *Perspective on Teaching*. Englewood Cliffs, N. J.: Prentice-Hall, Inc., 1961, pp. xvi and 432.

What Shall the High Schools Teach. 1956 Yearbook, Association for Supervision and Curriculum Development, pp. ix and 230.

WICKISER, RALPH L. *An Introduction to Art Education*. Yonkers, New York, World Book Co., 1957, pp. x and 342.

WINSLOW, LEON L. *Art in Secondary Education*. New York: McGraw-Hill Book Co., Inc., 1941, pp. xvii and 396.

Appendices

State Art Guides

1.	Alabama	None
2.	Alaska	None
3.	Arizona	None
4.	Arkansas	No information
5.	California	None
6.	Colorado	None
7.	Connecticut	None
8.	Delaware	None
9.	Florida	None
10.	Georgia	None, planned
11.	Hawaii	Art Teaching Guide, K-12, 1960, pp. 310, $4.00
12.	Idaho	Art Study Guide, 1-12, $1.00
13.	Illinois	None, planned
14.	Indiana	Digest of Courses of Study, 1961, pp. 320
15.	Iowa	No. XIII Art, Secondary, 1949, pp. 79, $ .75
16.	Kansas	None
17.	Kentucky	"Art Education," 1959, pp. 75, no charge
18.	Louisiana	Summary of the Art Education Program, 1959, pp. 6, no charge
19.	Maine	None
20.	Maryland	None
21.	Massachusetts	None
22.	Michigan	None
23.	Minnesota	A Guide for Instruction in Art, 1948, pp. 79, $1.60
24.	Mississippi	None
25.	Missouri	Art for Missouri: A Curriculum Guide for Grades 7, 8, and 9, 1960, pp. 234, no charge
26.	Montana	None
27.	Nebraska	No information

28.	Nevada	Suggested Art Program for Nevada's Schools, 1950, $1.00
29.	New Hampshire	In process
30.	New Jersey	None
31.	New Mexico	"The Child Creates," Art Guide, Grades 1-8, $1.50
32.	New York	"Art Education, Grades 7, 8, 9," 1957, pp. 30, $ .15, High School syllabus under revision
33.	North Carolina	"Art in the Public Schools," Grades 1-12, $ .50
34.	North Dakota	Art Course of Study, 1959, pp. 157, $1.50
35.	Ohio	None
36.	Oklahoma	No information
37.	Oregon	Out of print
38.	Pennsylvania	Course of Study in Art Education, 1951, $1.00
39.	Rhode Island	None
40.	South Carolina	No information
41.	South Dakota	None
42.	Tennessee	None, planned
43.	Texas	Curriculum Studies, Report #6, 1959, pp. 34, no charge
44.	Utah	Not available
45.	Vermont	None
46.	Virginia	Art and Youth, 1955, pp. 165, $2.00
47.	Washington	Art Guide, Grades 1-8, $2.50
48.	West Virginia	No information
49.	Wisconsin	"Art in the Total School Program," Bulletin #9, 1947, pp. 16, no charge
50.	Wyoming	None

City School District Art Guides*

1. New York, New York—"Art—Grades 7, 8, 9, and 10," 1955, pp. 184, $1.50; and "Major Art in the Academic High Schools," 1960, pp. 338, $3.00
2. Chicago, Illinois—"Teaching Guide for Arts," Grades K-14, $1.25
3. Los Angeles, California—"Ways to Art," 1952, $1.00; and "Instructional Guide for Senior High School Art," 1961, pp. 210
4. Philadelphia, Pennsylvania—under revision
5. Detroit, Michigan—none
6. Baltimore, Maryland—"Art Resource Materials for Secondary Schools," 1953, pp. 178, no charge
7. Houston, Texas—under revision
8. Cleveland, Ohio—none
9. Washington, D.C.—none
10. St. Louis, Missouri—no information
11. San Francisco, California—none
12. Milwaukee, Wisconsin—"Block Printing," Grade 9, 1957, pp. 21, $ .75; "Color," Grade 9, 1959, pp. 13, $ .50; "Design," Grade 9, 1960, pp. 25, $ .75; and "Single Stroke Lettering," Grade 9, 1956, pp. 12, $ .40
13. Boston, Massachusetts—"Course of Study in Art, J.H.S.," pp. 109, $ .30; "Course of Study in Art, H.S.," pp. 42, $ .90
14. Dallas, Texas—"Art Education" (Curriculum Guide), "Art Education" (Resource Materials), $2.55, $3.06
15. New Orleans, Louisiana—"A Program of Art—Junior High Schools," $1.75
16. Pittsburgh, Pennsylvania—"Guide to Art Activities" (available to district personnel only)
17. San Antonio, Texas—None
18. San Diego, California—"Art, 7th Grade, Guide for Teaching," 1961, pp. 32, $1.00; "Art, Manual for Teaching," 1961, pp. 35, $1.00; and "Art 1-2, Guide for," 1959 revision, 1961, pp. 36, $1.00

* Cities with a population of 250,000 and over.

19. Seattle, Washington—six one-page guides, $ .05 each and "Art is for Everyone," pp. 8, no charge (supplement to "Seattle Schools")
20. Buffalo, New York—None
21. Cincinnati, Ohio—"Art Education, Grades 7-9," 1958, pp. 169, $3.00
22. Memphis, Tennessee—"Art, Grades 7-12," $ .30
23. Denver, Colorado—"Creative Art in the Secondary School," $4.00 and 10 additional mimeographed pamphlets on specific media
24. Atlanta, Georgia—under revision
25. Minneapolis, Minnesota—"Exploratory Experiences and Resources in Art for Junior and Senior High School Students," 1960, $3.00 and "Guide to Teaching Graphic Arts, Grades 7-12," 1961, $2.50
26. Indianapolis, Indiana—"Art Experiences—K-8," 1952, pp. 80, $1.25 and "Art in Junior High Schools, Grades 7, 8, 9," 1955, pp. 80, $3.00
27. Kansas City, Missouri—none
28. Columbus, Ohio—"Tentative Teaching Guide for Fine Arts in the Secondary Schools," 1959, pp. 52, $ .50
29. Phoenix, Arizona—no information
30. Newark, New Jersey—"Art Guides, Junior and Senior High Schools," 1958, pp. 47, $1.00
31. Louisville, Kentucky—none
32. Portland, Oregon—"Guide to Art, General," $ .55 and 21 guides on specific media and bibliographies for secondary art
33. Oakland, California—none
34. Fort Worth, Texas—none
35. Long Beach, California—"Guide to Art in the Junior High School," mimeographed 1950; "Drawing and Painting in the Senior High School," mimeographed 1946, reissued 1950; "Guide to the Teaching of Art in the Senior High School," offset lithographed: Part I: Exploring Art, 1956; Part II: Constructive Arts, 1956; Part III: Home and Community Planning, 1956; Part IV: Stage Arts, 1959
36. Birmingham, Alabama—none
37. Oklahoma City, Oklahoma—in process
38. Rochester, New York—"A Guide in Elective Art for Secondary Schools," 1958, $1.30; Bulletin—A Seventh Grader Looks at Art, 1956, $ .25; Bulletin—Motivating and Inspiring Art Activities in Secondary Schools, 1957, $ .30; Bulletin—New Approaches to Design, Eighth Grade, 1956, $ .25; Display, 1960, $ .35
39. Toledo, Ohio—none
40. St. Paul, Minnesota—no information
41. Norfolk Virginia—"Exploratory Art," 1957, pp. 39; "Basic Art," 1957, pp. 35; and "Designing For Today," 1957, pp. 93, not for sale.
42. Omaha, Nebraska—no information
43. Honolulu, Hawaii—no information
44. Miami, Florida—none
45. Akron, Ohio—no information

46. El Paso, Texas—"Sourcebook for Arts and Handicraft," Grades 4-8, 1948, $2.50
47. Jersey City, New Jersey—no information
48. Tampa, Florida, no information
49. Dayton, Ohio—no information
50. Tulsa, Oklahoma—"Growth Through Art, Grades 7-12," 1960, pp. 66, $2.00
51. Wichita, Kansas—no information

Research in Secondary
Art Education

AROMI, EUGENE J. "Achievement of the Purposes of the Junior High School Through Experiences in the Plastic Arts." University of Alabama, 1960.

BAIN, ROBERT M. "An Analysis of Art Education in Oregon." University of Oregon, 1955.

BELSHE, FRANCIS B. "A History of Art Education in the Public Schools of the U. S." Yale University, 1946.

BLISS, WILLIAM H. "Photography in Secondary Schools: A Study of Photography in General Education with Special Emphasis on the Advantages of Its Integration with Industrial Arts Subjects." Bradley University, 1953.

BOND, GWENDOLINE M. "Outline of the History of Art for High School Students in the City of New York, with Suggestions to Teachers for Its Use." New York University, 1941.

BOSTWICK, PRUDENCE. "Providing for Esthetic Experience in Certaain Aspects of Secondary Education." Ohio State University, 1941.

BRAINARD, AMY GAMBLE. "An Analysis of Art Programs in Selected Junior High Schools in the United States." University of Southern California, 1955.

BROWN, KENNETH WILLIAM. "The Visual Arts in Secondary Education." Ohio State University, 1942.

BROWN, WILLIAM T. "The Relationship Between Popular-Unpopular Pictorial Subject Matter and Art Achievement at the Junior High School Level." Pennsylvania State University, 1962.

BURKHART, ROBERT C. "An Analysis of Individuality of Art Expression at the Senior High School Level." Pennsylvania State University, 1957.

BURLEY, FRANCES J. "Planning Facilities for Secondary Art Rooms." Columbia University, 1955.

CAMPBELL, MERRILL G. "A Study of Scholastic Accomplishment in Secondary School Fine Arts in Relation to Pupils' Relative Preference for This Subject." University of Pittsburgh, 1956.

CHANDLER, ANNA C. "Audio-Visual Enrichment of Art, Language Arts, and the Social Studies, a Handbook for Teachers of the Junior High Schools and for Teachers In-Training in New York City and the Metropolitan Area." New York University, 1943.

CLUBINE, GORDON L. "A Plan for the Improvement and Extension of Art Education in Ontario Secondary Schools." Columbia University, 1952.

CLUBINE, MARY H. "Effective Procedures in the Teaching of Art in Ontario Secondary Schools." Columbia University, 1952.

CONRAD, GEORGE. "A Plan for Art Education in the Secondary Schools." Columbia University, 1949.

COURTNEY, JOHN E. "Recommendations for Programs in Art Education Based Upon Statements of Secondary School Students." Columbia University, 1952.

CRESPI, DAVID E. "A Study of the Role of Early Adolescent Reality for Art Education in the Junior High School." Columbia University, 1959.

CULLEN, JAMES H. "How Secondary School Art Students Can Participate in School-Community Activities." New York University, 1955.

DENISTON, ROSS C. "Planning Art Facilities for Secondary Schools." Stanford University, 1956.

ESTEROS, GERTRUDE A. "Art Education for Home and Family Living." Columbia University, 1958.

FITZGERALD, JOHN B. "Factors Influencing Crafts Practices in Junior High School Art and Industrial Arts Programs." University of Connecticut, 1960.

FRANKSTON, LEON. "Some Explorations of the Effect of Creative Visual Art Experiences Upon the Poetry Writing Quality of Eighth Grade Students." Columbia University, 1963.

GAITSKELL, CHARLES D. "Art Education in the Province of Ontario." University of Toronto (Canada), 1947.

GATES, GERALD F. "The Enrichment of the Junior High School Art Program Through the Creative Use of Free and Inexpensive Materials." Denver University, 1955.

GAYNE, CLIFTON A., JR. "A Study of Art Programs in Selected Schools in Minnesota." University of Minnesota, 1947.

GLEASON, JOHN W. "A Design of Shared Services for Esthetic Development in the Schools and Communities of Lewis County in the State of New York." Columbia University, 1956.

GREEN, HARRY B. "The Introduction of Art as a General Education Subject in American Schools." Stanford University, 1948.

GREEN, LEAH A. "A Study of Creativity and the Self-Attitudes and Sociability of High School Students." Columbia University, 1957.

GROSLAND, AUGUST J. "The Content of Art Courses in High Schools of the U. S." University of Missouri, 1963.

GUNN, RICHARD L. "Effectiveness of Art Teachers in Meeting the Needs of Adolescents." Stanford University, 1956.

HADDOW, BURRITT J. "The Formulation of an Outline Guide of Background Information for the Teaching of the Fine Arts Content of the Tenth Year Course in World Institutions in the Social Studies Program in New York State." New York University, 1949.

HARRISON, CLEOBELLE. "A Study of the Trends in the Certification of Secondary School Teachers of Art and in the Objectives of Such Teaching." University of Michigan, 1952.

HOOVER, LOUIS. "Twentieth Century Art in America." (A Reference Book for the High School.) New York University, 1943.

JENSEN, LORRAINE L. "Art and the Adolescent: A Study of Certain Influences Affecting the Growth of Art Interests." Columbia University, 1959.

KLAEGER, MAX L. "A Comparative Study of the Preparation of Art Teachers, for American and German Secondary Schools." University of Minnesota, 1956.

LA CAFF, LEOLA M. "Art Interests and Experiences of Arizona High School Girls." University of California (Berkeley), 1952.

LANIER, VINCENT. "The Status of Current Objectives in Art Education: A Study of the Current Objectives of Public Art Education in Terms of the Values of Art Activities." New York University, 1954.

LEATHERBURY, LEVIN C. "Art Education in the Public Schools of Baltimore, Maryland: A Study of the History, Current Program, and Emerging Emphasis for Future Development." Columbia University, 1956.

MATTIL, EDWARD L. "A Study to Determine the Relationship Between Creative Products of Children, Ages 11-14, and Their Adjustment." Pennsylvania State University, 1953.

McCOY, ROBERT A. "A Course of Study for Secondary School Crafts." Oregon State University, 1953.

MICHAEL, JOHN A. "The Effect of Award, Adult Standard, and Peer Standard Upon the Creativeness in Art of High School Pupils." Pennsylvania State University, 1959.

MILLS, FREDERICK V. "A Study of the Precepts and Preferences Developed in Art Classes in Selected Indiana Schools." Indiana University, 1956.

MOORE, ALFRED H. "Practices and Opinions Relative to Practical Arts Education for Mentally Retarded Secondary School Youth." University of Missouri, 1954.

MORENO, JOSÉ A. "Art Curriculm for the Junior High Schools of Puerto Rico." University of Colorado, 1945.

NORTHCUTT, HELEN L. "Art Experiences and Interests of Selected Groups of Adolescents." University of Missouri, 1959.

OLSEN, JOHN. "Planning and Preparation of High School Yearbooks." Columbia University, 1949.

RICE, CHARLES M. "Methods and Materials for Teaching Photography in Secondary Schools." Oregon State University, 1958.

Rios, John F. "History of Art Education in the Secondary Schools of the United States from 1900-1950." University of Texas, 1954.

Schnyder, Dorothy M. "The Essential Elements in the Preparation of Teachers of Art for the Secondary Schools." New York University, 1936.

Shroff, Piroja D. "Seventh Grade Art Curriculum and Instruction in the Public Schools of Los Angeles County." University of Southern California, 1961.

Silverman, Ronald H. "Comparing the Effects of Two Versus Three-Dimensional Art Activity Upon Spatial Visualization, Aesthetic Judgment, and Art Interest." Stanford University, 1962.

Slockbower, Edward W. "The Initiation of a Creative Arts Program in a Situation Based Upon Competitive Scholarship and a Uniform Manual Arts Course." Columbia University, 1943.

Smith, Arthur E. "Evaluative Criteria for the Non-Instructional Aspects of the High School Art Program." Syracuse University, 1953.

Teed, Truman Henry. "The Relationship of the Two-Dimensional and Three-Dimensional Creative Art Expressions of the Adolescent." Pennsylvania State University, 1962.

Tobin, David. "Art Experiences for the Maladjusted Adolescent." New York University, 1957.

Uhlin, Donald M. "The Effect of Adolescent Physical Development on Art Expression." Pennsylvania State University, 1953.

Waterman, Edward C. "The Development of a National Monthly Art Newspaper for Junior and Senior High School Students." New York University, 1962.

Weiley, Earl A. "Socio-Economic Influences in the Development of American Art Education in the Nineteenth Century." Michigan State University, 1957.

Wilding, John H. "Art Education in High School as It Affects Home and Family Living." University of Southern California, 1960.

Wilson, Delius E. "Factors Related to the Teaching of Art in a Junior High School in a Low Socio-Economic District of an Urban Community." Columbia University, 1960.

Winsand, Orville M. "Art Appreciation in the Public Schools From 1930 to 1960." University of Wisconsin, 1961.

Wyckoff, Donald L. "A Report on an Experiment in Relating the Arts at Pascack Valley Regional High School in Hillsdale, New Jersey." Columbia University, 1962.

Index

INDEX

DATE DUE

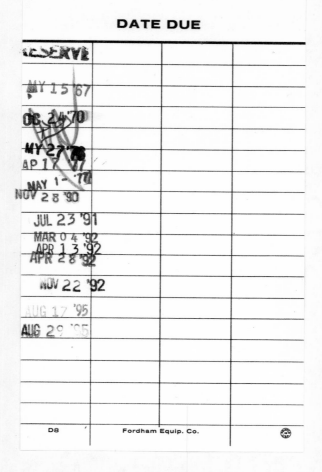

RESERVE			
MY 15 '67			
OC 24 '70			
MY 27 '76			
AP 17 '77			
MAY 1 - '70			
NOV 28 '90			
JUL 23 '91			
MAR 0 4 '92			
APR 1 3 '92			
APR 2 8 '92			
NOV 22 '92			
AUG 17 '95			
AUG 29 '95			
D8	Fordham Equip. Co.		